THE FLOWING BOWL

THE

FLOWING BOWL

A TREATISE ON DRINKS OF ALL KINDS AND OF -
ALL PERIODS, INTERSPERSED WITH SUNDRY
ANECDOTES AND REMINISCENCES

BY

EDWARD SPENCER

('NATHANIEL GUBBINS')

AUTHOR OF 'CAKES AND ALE,' ETC.

London

GRANT RICHARDS

PREFACE

I CLAIM no merit for the following pages, other than may attach to industry, application, the gift of copying accurately, and the acquisition of writer's cramp. The mechanical writing is—to the great joy of the compositors who have dealt with it—every letter mine own ; but the best part of the book has been conveyed from other sources. In fact the book is, as the old lady said of the divine tragedy of *Hamlet*, "full of quotations." The hand is the hand of Gubbins, but the voice is, for the most part, the voice of the great ones of the past, including Pliny and Gervase Markham. The matter, or most of it—I am endeavouring to drive the fact home—is culled from other sources ; and if this is the most useful and interesting work ever published it is more my fortune than my fault.

The genial reception of my earlier effort, *Cakes and Ale*—which was condemned only by worshippers of *Ala*, who were not expected to applaud—together with the hope of earning

something towards the purchase of a Bath Chair
—have induced me to issue this little treatise on
liquids, as a companion to my first cloth-bound
book. And innate modesty—I stick to "innate," despite the critics—compels me to add
that I think the last is the better work. I will,
however, leave a generous and discriminating
public to decide that question for itself.

LONDON, CHRISTMAS EVE, 1898.

CONTENTS

CHAPTER I

THE OLD ADAM

CHAPTER II

MORE FRIGHTFUL EXAMPLES

CHAPTER III

DRINKS ANCIENT AND MODERN

CHAPTER IV

SOME OLD RECIPES

CONTENTS ix

CHAPTER V

GLORIOUS BEER

CHAPTER VI

ALL ALE

CHAPTER VII

A SPIRITUOUS DISCOURSE

CHAPTER VIII

OTHER SPIRITS

CHAPTER IX

CUPS WHICH CHEER

CHAPTER X

PUNCH

CHAPTER XI

STRANGE SWALLOWS

CHAPTER XII

" THE BOY "

CHAPTER XIII

THE OLD WINES AND THE NEW

CHAPTER XIV

THE LONG AND THE SHORT OF IT

CHAPTER XV

STILL HARPING ON THE DRINK

CHAPTER XVI

" APPLE SASS "

CHAPTER XVII

CORDIALS AND LIQUEURS

CHAPTER XVIII

THE AFTERMATH OF REVELRY

CHAPTER XIX

THE DRINKS OF DICKENS

CHAPTER XX

SWORN OFF !

CHAPTER I

THE OLD ADAM

Introductory—Awful habits of the ancients—A bold, bad book—
Seneca on the Drink Habit—The bow must not be always
strung—*Ebrietatis Encomium*—The noble Romans—"Dum
vivimus vivamus"—The skeleton at the banquet—Skull-
cups—"Life and wine are the same thing"—Virgil and his
contemporaries—Goats for Bacchus—The days of Pliny—
Rewards for drunkenness — Novellius Torquatus — Three
gallons at a draught—A swallow which did not save Rome
—The antiquity of getting for'ard—Noah as a grape-grower
—Father Frassen's ideas—Procopius of Gaza—New Testament wine—Fermented or not?—Bad old Early Christians
—Drunkenness common in Africa—Religion a cloak for
alcohol—Tertullian on cider—Paulinus excuses intemperance—Excellence of Early Christians' intentions.

I WISH to state at the outset that this little work
is not compiled in the interests of the sot, the
toper, and the habitual over-estimator of his
swallowing capacity.   That the gifts of the
gods, and the concoctions of more or less vile
man, should be used with moderation, if we wish
to really and thoroughly enjoy them, is a truism
which needs no repetition ; and although at the
commencement of this work many " frightful

B

examples " of the evils of over-indulgence will be found mentioned, nothing but moderation will be found counselled in my book, from cover to cover.

In the past, drunkenness was not always regarded as a vice, and this is evident from much of the literature of former generations. In the course of my researches into the alcohol question I have come across a little book which bears the shameful and abandoned title of *Ebrietatis En-comium, or the Praise of Drunkenness*. And this book, which conveys such questionably moral aphorisms as " It is good for one's health to be drunk occasionally," and " The truly happy are the truly intoxicated," claims to prove, " most authentically and most evidently, the necessity of frequently getting drunk, and that the practice is most ancient, primitive, and catholic."

The author commences with what he calls " a beautiful passage out of Seneca :—

" The soul must not be always bent: one must sometimes allow it a little pleasure. Socrates was not ashamed to pass the time with children. Cato enjoyed himself in drinking plentifully, when his mind had been too much wearied out in public affairs. Scipio knew very well how to move that body, so much inured to wars and triumphs, without breaking it, as some nowadays do . . . ; but as people did in past times, who would make themselves merry on their festivals, by leading a dance really worthy men of those days, whence could ensue no reproach, when even their very enemies had seen them dance. One must allow the mind

some recreation : it makes it more gay and
peaceful. . . . Assiduity of labour begets a
languor and bluntness of the mind : for sleep is
very necessary to refresh us, and yet he that
would do nothing else but sleep night and day
would be a dead man, and no more. There
is a great deal of difference between loosening
a thing, and quite unravelling it. Those who
made laws have instituted holidays, to oblige
people to appear at public rejoicings, in order to
mingle with their cares a necessary temperament.
. . . You must sometimes walk in the open air,
that the mind may exalt itself by seeing the
heavens, and breathing the air at your ease ;
sometimes take the air in your chariot, the roads
and the change of the country will re-establish
you in your vigour ; or you may eat and drink
a little more plentifully than usual. Sometimes
one must even go as far as to get drunk ; not
indeed with an intention to drown ourselves in
wine, but to drown our care. For wine drives
away sorrow and care, and goes and fetches them
up from the bottom of the soul. And as
drunkenness cures some distempers, so, in like
manner, it is a sovereign remedy for our sorrows "
(Seneca *de Tranquillitate*).

Such sentiments were doubtless popular
enough in Great Britain at the commencement
of the present century — when *Ebrietatis En-
comium* was published — when three and four
bottle-men slept where they fell, "repugnant to
command " ; and malt liquor, small or strong,
was the only known matutinal restorative of
manly vigour. But my own experience is that

the sorrow and care which may be temporarily
driven away by drowning them in the bowl are
apt to return within a very few hours, reinforced
an hundredfold, with their weapons re-sharpened,
their instruments of torture put in thorough
working-order, and with many other devils worse
than themselves. A man, sound in body and
mind, may really enjoy a certain amount of good
liquor without feeling any ill effects next morning ; but woe to him who seeks to drown that
which cannot sink ; to crush the worm which
knows not death ! The individual has yet to be
born who can flourish, either in body or soul,
on his own immoderation ; and but for a chronic
state of thirst in early youth I should not now
be reduced to the compilation of drink statistics
for a living.

But the ancients, in their heathen philosophy
—which, by the way, was once recommended to
Christians to follow—took no thought for the
morrow. " Carpe diem ! " was the head and
front of the programme of the Roman patricians,
who used to cry aloud at their feasts, by way of
grace before meat :—

Amici,
Dum Vivimus
Vivamus !

This was probably the original version of " We
won't go home till morning," and was sung, or
shouted, at all bean-feasts and smart supper-
parties. The ancient Egyptians made use of a
very extraordinary, and a very nasty, custom in
their festivals. They shewed to every guest a

skeleton, before the soup was served. This, according to some historians, was to make the feasters think on their latter end. But others assert that this strange figure was brought into use for a directly opposite reason ; that the image of death was shewn for no other intent than to excite the guests to pass their lives merrily, and to employ the few days of its small duration to the best advantage ; as having no other condition to expect after death than that of this frightful skeleton.

This was the idea of one Trimalchion, who, Petronius tells us, thus expressed himself on the subject : " Alas ! alas ! wretched that we are ! What a nothing is poor man ! We shall be like this, when Fate shall have snatched us hence. Let us therefore rejoice, and be merry while we are here." The original Latin of this translation is much stronger, and had better not be given here. And the same Trimalchion on another occasion remarked : " Alas ! Wine therefore lives longer than man, let us then sit down and drink bumpers ; life and wine are the same thing."

The Scythians undoubtedly used to drink out of vessels fashioned from human skulls, and probably had the same design in doing so as the Egyptians had in looking on their nasty skeletons.

In Virgil's time, his contemporaries—and very probably the old man himself—drank deep ; but instead of fighting, and breaking things, and jumping on their wives, and getting locked up, they brought their own heathen religion into their debaucheries. In more civilized circles, at this end of the most civilized century, the reveller

goes out "to see a man," and subsequently
"shouts for the crowd" ; but in Virgil's time
a man who had a drink was said to be "pouring
forth libations to the gods," "making sacrifices"
—more especially to Bacchus, the wine deity,
whom nothing under the slaughter of a he-goat
was supposed to propitiate. And the "Billy"
was chosen for the sacrifice, because the tender
shoots of the vine formed his favourite food, in
a land in which there was neither brown paper,
nor wall-plaster, nor salmon-tins, to nibble. And
these sacrifices to the rosy god were "occasions"
(as they say in the City) indeed ! I have often
wondered what the ancients did to cure a headache ; and whether a man said to be "possessed
of a devil" was in reality suffering from Alcohol,
"the Devil in solution," in the shape of *delirium
tremens* in one of its many and objectionable forms.

In the time of Pliny, drunkenness and
debauchery appear to have been the principal
studies of the nations about whom he had
information. A man was actually *rewarded* for
getting drunk—tell it not in Vine Street, W. !
The greatest drinker got the most prizes ; and
Pliny informs us that whilst the Parthians contended for the distinction of having the hardest
heads and the longest swallows, they were simply
"not in it" with the Milanese, who had a real
champion in one Novellius Torquatus. This
man, according to history, could have given a
market-porter of the present day, a brewer's
drayman, or a stockbroker, any amount of start
over the Alcohol course, and "lost" him.

This Novellius won the championship from all

pretenders, and "had gone through all honourable
degrees of dignity in Rome, wherein the greatest
repute he obtained was for drinking in the
presence of Tiberius three gallons of wine at one
draught, and before he drew his breath again ;
neither did he rest there, but he so far had
acquired the art of drinking, that although he continued at it, yet was never known to falter in his
tongue ; and were it ne'er so late in the evening
he followed this exercise, yet would be ready again
for it in the morning. Those large draughts also
he drank at one breath, without leaving in the cup
so much as would dash against the pavement."

Ah ! We have nobody up to this form to
talk about nowadays ; and if men have improved
in morality they must have deteriorated in
capacity, or the occupation of gaolers and warders
would be gone. And the poor old poet " Spring
Onions," with even a tenth part of the powers
of endurance and swallow of Novellius Torquatus,
might have escaped even one solitary conviction.

"If the antiquity of a custom," writes the
author of *Ebrietatis Encomium*, " makes it always
good and laudable, certainly · drunkenness can
never deserve sufficient recommendation. Every
one knows that Noah got drunk after he had
planted the vine. There are some who pretend
to excuse him, that he was not acquainted with
the strength of wine. But to this it may very
well be answered that it is not very probable so
wise a man as Noah should plant a vine without
knowing its nature and property. Besides it is one
thing to know whether he got drunk at all : and
another whether he had an intention to do so."

The amount of water previously experienced by Noah should surely be sufficient to purge him of the offence of making too free with the fruit of the vine !

"But," continues the laudator of ebriety, "if we give any credit to several learned persons, Noah was not the first man who got fuddled. Father Frassen maintains 'that people fed on flesh before the Flood, and drank wine.' There is no likelihood, according to him, that men contented themselves with drinking water for fifteen or sixteen hundred years together. It is much more credible that they prepared a drink more nourishing and palatable. These first men of the world were endued with no less share of wit than their posterity, and consequently wanted no industry to invent everything that might contribute to make them pass their lives agreeably. Before the Flood men married, and gave their children in marriage. These people regaled each other, and made solemn entertainments. Now who can imagine that they drank at those festivals nothing but water, and fed only on fruits and herbs ! Noah, therefore, was not the inventor of the use which we make of the grape ; the most that he did was only to plant new vines."

Procopius of Gaza, one of the most ancient and learned interpreters of Scripture, thinks it no less true that the vine was known in the world before Noah's time ; but he does not allow that the use of wine was known before the patriarch, whom he believes to be the inventor of it. As for the wine mentioned in the New Testament, we are now assured by modern commentators—total abstainers every one—that it was unfermented, devoid of alcohol, and non-intoxicating. I had certainly always looked upon the wine which Timothy was enjoined to take for his " stomach's sake," as some form of brandy.

The Early Christians—like far too many of the late ditto—were terrible topers. Ecclesiastical history tells us that in the primitive church it was customary to appoint solemn feasts on the festivals of martyrs. This appears by the harangue of Constantine, and from the works of St. Gregory Nazianzen, and St. Chrysostom. Drunkenness was rife at those feasts; and this excess was looked upon as permissible. This is shewn by the pathetic complaints of St. Augustine and St. Cyprian, the former of which holy fathers thus delivered himself:—

"Drunken debauches pass as permitted amongst us, so that people turn them into solemn feasts, to honour the memory of the martyrs; and that not only on those days which are particularly consecrated to them (which would be a deplorable abuse to those who look at those things with other eyes than those of the flesh), but on every day of the year."

St. Cyprian, in a treatise attributed to him, says much the same thing:—

"Drunkenness is so common with us in Africa that it scarce passes for a crime. And do we not see Christians forcing one another to get drunk, to celebrate the memory of the martyrs?"

Cardinal du Perron told his contemporaries "that the Manichæans said that the Catholicks were people much given to wine, but that they never drank any," which sounds paradoxical. Against this charge St. Augustine only defends them by recrimination. He answers, "that it was true, but that they (the Manichæans) drank the juice of apples, which was more delicious than all the wines and liquors in the world." And so does Tertullian, who said the liquor press'd from apples was most strong and vinous. His words are: "Succum ex pomis vinosissimum."

I trust that in quoting all those things I am not becoming wearisome, at the very commencement of my work; the main object being to show that all the drinking in the world is not done by the present generation of vipers.

But the Early Christians were excused for their habits of soaking, by Paulinus, on the grounds of the "excellence of their intentions"; which naturally reminds us of the celebrated excuse of the late Monsieur Thiers, on a much later occasion. The words of Paulinus are, when translated and adapted :—

But yet that mirth in little feasts enjoy'd
I think should ready absolution find ;
   Slight peccadillo of an erring mind,
Artless and rude, of all disguises void,
   Their simple hearts too easy to believe
(Conscious of nothing ill) that saints in tombs
   Enshrin'd should any happiness perceive
From quaffing cups, and wines' ascending fumes,
   Must be excus'd, since what they did they meant
With piety ill plac'd, yet good intent.

Similar pleas are occasionally urged by roysterers nowadays; yet they are but seldom credited in their own parishes.

CHAPTER II

NOT even popes, saints, or bishops were exempt
from accusations of loving the juice of the grape,
or of the apple, too well. We read in the
adages of Erasmus that it was a proverb amongst
the Germans that the lives of the monks consisted in nothing but eating and drinking.
One H. Stephens says on this subject, in his
apology for Herodotus :—

" But to return to these proverbs, theological
wine, and the abbot's, or prelate's, table. I say

that without these one could never rightly understand the beautiful passage of Horace :—

> Nunc est bibendum, nunc pede libero
> Pulsanda tellus ; nunc Saliaribus
> Ornare pulvinar Deorum
> Tempus erat dapibus sodales,

nor this other :—

> Absumet haeres Caecuba dignior
> Servata centum clavibus : et mero
> Tinget pavimentum superbo
> Pontificum potiore coenis."

Modern popes have always had a reputation for
abstemiousness ; but this same Mr. Stephens—
who must have been somewhat of a slander-
monger — in his same apology for Herodotus
(what about the apology for Stephens ?) mentions
a popular little song of the day, which commenced :—

> Le Pape qui est à Rome
> Boit du vin comme un autre homme,
> Et du l'Hypocras aussi.

And I can recall a cheery, albeit most likely
libellous, song, which some of us used to sing at
school, beginning :—

> The Pope he leads a joyous life.

It appears to be a fact that many former popes
drank hard ; and if Petrarch is to be believed,
the long stay made by the court of Rome at
Avignon was on account of the excellence of the
French wines ; and that it was merely for that

reason that they stayed so long in Provence, and removed with so much reluctance.

Now for the saints. Although the fact of his drinking deep has been denied, St. Augustine appears to have confessed to "a day out" occasionally, in some such words as these : " Thy servant has been sometimes crop-sick through excess of wine. Have mercy on me, that it may be ever far from me."

Amongst the bishops one instance must suffice. " Pontus de Thiard," as appears from an old translation of the works of an eminent Frenchman, "after having repented of the sins of his youth, came to be bishop of Chalons-sur-Soane ; but, however, he did not renounce the power of drinking heavily, which seemed then inseparable from the quality of a good poet. He had a stomach big enough to empty the largest cellar ; and the best wines of Burgundy were too gross for the subtility of the fire which devoured him. Every night, at going to bed, besides the ordinary doses of the day, in which he would not suffer the least drop of water, he used to drink a bottle before he slept. He enjoyed a strong, robust, and vigorous health, to the age of fourscore." Dear old Pontus !

Of all other mighty men, Alexander the Great serves to best point the moral of the evils of intemperance. Wearied of conquering, this hero gave himself up to debauchery in its worst and wildest forms. He killed his foster-brother in a fit of drunkenness, and subsequently, at the bidding of "lovely Thais," queen of the

Athenian *demi-monde*, set fire to, and burnt to
the ground, Persepolis, the wonder of the world.
What an awakening Alec must have had ! Not
that he was the first, nor yet the last, man to
make a fool, or rogue, of himself, at the bidding
of the (alleged) gentler sex. Cleopatra corrupted
a few heroes, and as for La Pompadour—— but
those be other stories. Alexander the Great,
who had lost most of his greatness by that time,
died from the effects of chronic alcoholism ;
although they didn't tell me as much as this at
school.

Cambyses was but little removed from a sot.
This prince, having been told by one of his
courtiers that the people thought Cambyses
indulged in too many " drunks " for the good of
the nation, reached for his best bow and his
sharpest arrow, and, the courtier having retired
out of range, shot the courtier's son through the
heart ; after which the prince enquired of the
courtier : " Is this the act of a drunkard ? "
which reminds me of a more modern anecdote,
of a Piccadilly roysterer. But some men can
shoot straighter, and ride better, and write more
poetically, when under the influence of the rosy
god ; and had this courtier been a man of the
world he would not have touched on the subject
of ebriation to his prince. For ebriates are but
seldom proud of their weaknesses.

Darius,the first King of Persia,commanded that
this epitaph, which is here translated, should be
placed on his tomb : " I could drink much wine
and bear it well." Philip of Macedon, father of
Alexander the Great, took too much wine on

occasion ; to corroborate · which fact we have
the exclamation of the good lady whose prayer
for justice he had refused to hear — this is a
quotation beloved of members of Parliament—
" I appeal from Philip drunk to Philip sober."
Dionysius the younger, tyrant of Sicily, frequently had vine-leaves in his hair for a week at
a time ; he drank himself almost blind, and his
courtiers, in order to flatter him, pretended to be
blind too, and neither ate nor drank anything
unless it were handed to them by Dionysius
himself. Tiberius was called Biberius, because
of his excessive attachment to the bowl ; and, in
derision, they changed his surname of Nero to
Mero. Bonosus, according to his own historian,
Flavius Vobiscus, was a terrible soaker, and used
to make the ambassadors, who came from foreign
parts, even more drunk than himself, in order
that he might discover their secret instructions.

I cannot glean from the ancient records that
any monarch who reigned over Great Britain
was an habitual drunkard, an absolute and con-
firmed sot. But many of them were given to
conviviality, notably Richard of the Lion Heart,
Bluff King Hal — who had gout badly, and
suffered also from obesity and other things—and
the Merry Monarch. A story is told of the
Second Charles, that when dining with the Lord
Mayor, Sir Robert Viner, on one occasion—it
was probably a 9th of November dinner at the
Mansion House—the King noticed that most of
the guests were uncomfortably uproarious, and,
with his suite, rose to leave the banqueting
chamber. Whereupon the Lord Mayor hastily

pursued him, caught hold of his robe, and exclaimed : " Sire, you shall take t'other bottle."
The King stopped, and with a graceful smile
repeated a line of the old song, " He that is drunk
is great as a king," and with this compliment to
his host, he returned, and took " t'other bottle."

The immortal Pepys describes a Lord Mayor's
Feast which was given in 1663. It was served
at one o'clock, and a bill of fare was placed,
together with a salt-cellar, in front of every
guest ; whilst at the end of each table was a list
of " persons proper " there to be seated. Pepys
was placed at the merchant-strangers' table,
" where ten good dishes to a mess, with plenty
of wine of all sorts." Napkins and knives were,
however, only supplied at the Lord Mayor's table
to him and the Lords of the Privy Council ; and
Pepys complains bitterly that he and those who
were seated with him had no napkins nor change
of trenchers, and had to drink out of earthen
pitchers. He, however, took his spoon and fork
away with him, as was customary in those days
with all guests invited to entertainments. But
as each guest brought his own tools, nobody was
the worse for this custom. The dinner, says
Pepys, was provided by the Mayor and two
sheriffs for the time being, and the whole cost
was between £700 and £800.

We are not told what was drunk at the
Mansion House on that occasion, but I have a
list before me of the potables served at the Lord
Mayor's banquet in 1782—more than a century
later—which seems deserving of mention in this
little work :—

Port	.	.	.	. 438	bottles
Lisbon		.	.	. 220	,,
Madeira		.	.	. 90	,,
Claret		.	.	. 168	,,
Champagne			.	. 143	,,
Burgundy	.		.	. 116	,,
Malmsey, or Sack			.	4	,,
Brandy		.	.	4	,,
Hock	.	.	.	. 66	,,

Grand Total   . 1249   ,,

There be several remarkable features in the above list. I had imagined that a taste for claret had not been fully acquired by the British rate-payer until some years later than this ; whilst the virtues of champagne could not have been fully recognized. Lisbon, I conceive to have been another sort of port, and this seems to have been neck-and-cork above all other vintages in popular favour. The taste for such mawkish stuff as malmsey must have been at vanishing point ; whilst one is led to ask what, with only such a minute allowance of sack, did these feasters drink with their soup ? Was the succulency of calipash and calipee known in those days ; and if so, where was the harmless necessary milk-punch ? But the most remarkable feature of all in the above catalogue is the meagre allowance of brandy for the crowd. The parable of the loaves and fishes would not appear more miraculous than that, in these later days, a multitude could be filled, after a big dinner, with *four* bottles of cognac ! And this despite the fact of whisky having almost entirely usurped the place of the other strong-water.

One hundred years ago, to be "drunk as a lord" was considered the height of human happiness. And at this period the Church had not severed its old connection with alcohol. In fact intemperance was encouraged by our pastors and masters; and in certain districts of England the churchwardens, at Whitsuntide, made collections of malt from the parishioners, and this was brewed into strong ale, and sold in the churches, the money so obtained being expended on the repairs of the sacred edifices; and it was a frequent and a saddening spectacle to see men who had drunk not wisely reeling about the aisles. Until as late as 1827—in which year the license was withdrawn—a church and a tavern were covered by the same roof, in the parish of Deepdale, a village between Derby and Nottingham; and a door which could be opened at will led from the altar to the tap-room.

A Romish priest wrote in praise of the bowl as follows :—

Si bene commemini, causae sunt quinque bibendi :
Hospitis adventus ; praesens sitis ; atque futura ;
Aut vini bonitas ; aut quaelibet altera causa.

Which comforting and jovial sentiments were thus adapted for the use of colleges and private bars, by Dean Aldrich, D.D., the great master of logic at Oxford :—

There are, if I do rightly think,
Five reasons why a man should drink :
Good wine, a friend, or being dry,
Or lest you should be by and by——
Or any other reason why.

But after all no nation ever did themselves so well, in the matter of wines, as the inhabitants of bad old ancient Rome.

" It was to excess of drinking," wrote Whyte Melville, in *The Gladiators*, " that the gluttons of that period looked as the especial relief of every entertainment ; since the hope of each seemed to be that when thoroughly flooded, and so to speak washed out with wine, he might begin eating again. The Roman was no drunkard, like the barbarian, for the sake of that wild excitement of the brain which is purchased by intoxication. No, he ate to repletion that he might drink in gratification. He drank to excess that he might eat again."

Further on the same writer remarks : "Whilst marvelling at the quantity of wine consumed by the Romans in their entertainments, we must remember that it was the pure and unadulterated juice of the grape, that it was in general freely mixed with water, and that they imbibed but a very small portion of alcohol, which is the destructive quality of all stimulants."

As to the Roman vintages being "in general freely mixed with water," I have grave doubts. I have an idea that Maecenas would have made it particularly warm for that slave who might have dared to water his old Falernian ; and, take them altogether, an amusement-loving, and playgoing public, for whom the legitimate drama took the form of certain brave men and fair women being torn and eaten by wild beasts, would hardly have been content with such drink for babes as " claret cold."

Ancient poets were not less backward than modern votaries of the muses ; and it is related of the poet Philoxenus that he was frequently heard to express the wish that he had a neck as long as a crane's, that he might the longer have the pleasure of swallowing wine, and of enjoying its delicious taste.   I have heard the same wish expressed, during much more recent years.

One more old song, translated from a French *chanson à boire*, and I take my leave of the awful habits of the ancients (I trust) for ever.   It is called

THE TIPPLING PHILOSOPHERS.

Diogenes, surly and proud,
Who snarl'd at the Macedon youth,
Delighted in wine that was good,
  Because in good wine there is truth ;
  But growing as poor as a Job,
    Unable to purchase a flask,
  He chose for his mansion a tub,
    And lived by the scent of the cask.

[Neither the air, nor the chorus, of this song is given in the old MS.   But I would suggest the old air of "Wednesbury Cocking," with a little "tol-de-rol" at the finish of each verse.]

Heraclitus ne'er could deny
To tipple and cherish his heart,
And when he was maudlin he'd cry,
  Because he had empty'd his quart ;
  Tho' some are so foolish to think
    He wept at men's folly and vice,
  'Twas only his fashion to drink
    Till the liquor flow'd out of his eyes.

Democritus always was glad
Of a bumper to cheer up his soul,
And would laugh like a man that was mad
When over a good flowing bowl.
As long as his cellar was stor'd,
The liquor he'd merrily quaff,
And when he was drunk as a lord
At those who were sober he'd laugh.

Aristotle, the master of arts,
Had been but a dunce without wine,
And what we ascribe to his parts
Is due to the juice of the vine.
His belly most writers agree
Was as big as a watering trough,
He therefore leap'd into the sea,
Because he'd have liquor enough.

Old Plato, the learned divine,
He fondly to wisdom was prone,
But had it not been for good wine,
His merits had never been known ;
By wine we are generous made,
It furnishes fancy with wings,
Without it we ne'er should have had
Philosophers, poets, or kings.

CHAPTER III

DRINKS ANCIENT AND MODERN

The Whitaker of the period—France without wine—Babylonian
boozers—Beer discovered by the Egyptians—A glass of bitter
for Cleopatra—Brainless Persians—German sots—Turning
the tables—Intemperance in the North—Chinese intoxicants
—Nature of Sack—Mead and morat—Vinous metheglin—
Favourite tipple of the Ancient Britons—Braggonet—Birch-
wine — "The invariable" of Falstaff — A recipe by Sir
Walter Raleigh — Saragossa wine—Usquebaugh—Clary—
Apricock wine.

PLINY—whose works contain almost as much
general information as Whitaker's Almanack—
tells us that the western nations got drunk with
certain liquors made with fruits ; and that those
liquors have different names in Gaul and Spain,
though they produce the same effect.   Ammianus
Marcellinus reports that " the Gauls having no
wine in their country " — only fancy what a
country France must have been to live in without champagne and claret, not to mention
burgundy and cider — " though they are very
fond of it, contrive a great many sorts of liquors
which produce the same effect as wine."   The
Scythians, too, had no wine, but got " for'ard "

just the same. One of their philosophers, upon being asked if they had nobody who played the flute in Scythia, replied that " they had not so much as any wine there." Which seems to hint to flute-playing being a thirsty trade, even in those days.

The Babylonians were, according to Herodotus, habitual over - estimators of their swallowing capacity, and got merry after inhaling the fumes of certain herbs which they burned ; which sounds like anything but a comfortable debauch, and must have choked some of them. Strabo tells all who care to read him that the Indians drank the juice of sugar-canes, which we now call rum ; whilst according to Pliny and Athenaeus the Egyptians fuddled themselves with a drink made from barley ; evidently undeveloped beer. And it is quite on the cards that Cleopatra occasionally drew, with her own fair hands, for her beloved Antony, a glass of " bitter," with a head on it.

But the quaintest and most awe-inspiring of all drinks seems to have been that affected by the Persians — now decent, sober people enough ; this was a liquor made from boiled poppy-seeds, and called

Kokemaar.

They drank it scalding hot, in the presence of many spectators, who may or may not have been charged for admission.

" Before it operates," wrote a chronicler of the times, " they quarrel with one another, and give abusive language, without coming to blows ; afterwards when the drug begins to have its

effect, then they also begin to make peace. One
compliments in a very high degree, another tells
stories, but all are extremely ridiculous both in
their words and actions." And after mentioning
other liquors which they use, he adds, "It is
difficult to find in Persia a man that is not
addicted to one of these liquors, without which
they think they cannot live but very unpleasantly."
Anything nastier than hot laudanum as a restorative I cannot imagine.

It sounds curious to read that France and
Spain were censured by that universal provider of
knowledge, Pliny, for their drunkenness with
beer and ale, "wines not being in that age so
frequent." What was the world like before the
invention of port wine, I wonder? For in
Pliny's time Italy exceeded all parts of the world
for her luscious and curious vintages, being responsible for 195 different sorts of wines.

Their Names and Kinds innumerable are,
Nor for their Catalogue we need not care ;
Which who would know as soon may count the
      Sands
The *Western* Winds raise on the *Libyan* Strands.

At a much later date, in the seventeenth
century, Italy still held her own in the matter of
the juice of the grape ; and then, as now, their
Chianti and Lachrymae Christi were justly celebrated. Strange to say at the same period the
Germans, we read, "are much given to drunkenness, as one of their own countrymen writes of
them ; they drink so immodestly and immoderately
at their Banquets that they cannot pour their beer

in fast enough with the ordinary Quaffing Cups, but drink in large Tankards whole draughts, none to be left under severe penalties ; admiring him that will drink most, and hating him that will not pledge them."

I once, in my salad days, assisted in the attempt to make a German " foxed." There were some half a dozen of us, nice boys all, and we entertained this Teuton right royally. At the banquet table the champagne was decanted, and it was so arranged that our guest should imbibe at least twice as much as anybody else. Then we took him around the great city. At four the next morning the German sat facing me in the smoking-room of a little social club. Everybody else had gone home, more or less limp, or had come to anchor in some police-station. And I did not feel very well myself. And as the clock chimed four, and the grey dawn stole in through the venetians in streaks, that German uprose in all his majesty—he was six feet five inches and broad in proportion—smote me hard on the back, and enquired, in cheerful tones : " Now then ! Vhere can ve go to haf some fun ? " We never " took on " any more of the children of the Fatherland.

The Russians, Swedes, Danes, and other Northerners—also during the seventeenth century —we read, " exceed all the rest, having made the drinking of Brandy, Aqua Vitae, Hydromel, Beer, Mum, Meth, and other liquors in great quantities, so familiar to them that they usually drink our countrymen to death."

" The Mahometans," the same writer tells us,

"which possess a great part of the world, on a
superstitious account forbear the drinking of
much wine ; because that a young and beautiful
woman being accosted by two angels, that had
intoxicated themselves with it "—an intoxicated
angel surely takes the cake ? — "taking the
advantage of their ebriety, made her escape, and
was for her beauty and wit prefer'd in Heaven,
and the angels severely punished for their folly ;
for which reason they are commanded not to
drink wine. Yet many of them, doubting of
the divinity of that relation, do transgress that
command, and liberally drink of the blood of the
grape, which the Christians prepare out of their
own vineyards ; palliating their crime, in that
they did not plant the tree, nor make the wine."
For the philosophy of the Mahomedan is like the
ways of the Heathen Chinee, "peculiar."

"The Chineses," we are further told, "are
the least addicted to ebriety, delighting themselves in Coffee, Tea, and such like drinks, free
from those stupifying qualities ; yet are they not
without their carouses ; and those of the intoxicating drinks prepared of Rice, Coco's, Sugar,
Dates, etc., equalling in strength and spirit any
liquors in the world."

With the "Chineses" must be of course included the gallant little Japaneses, with which
nation English chroniclers had but a slight acquaintance three hundred years ago.

Without enquiring too closely into the nature
of Red Falernian, Coan, Massic, or any of the
Roman vintages at the time of dear old Horatius
Flaccus, let us take a glance over the wine-lists

of our own country, from the Saxon period. And the first thing which will naturally strike the observer is the heavy, loaded nature of their dinner drinks. A little later on, Sack did duty for the "inferior sherry" of the Victorian era, although a Sack-and-Angostura was not a frequent demand amongst the young bloods of the period. On the festive boards of the Saxons appeared, besides ale of the strongest and cider of the roughest, home-made wines, mead, morat, metheglin, and more or less odoriferous pigments. In case any enterprising ratepayer should elect to give his guests

Mead,

at his next house-warming, here is the ancient recipe.

Take of spring-water what quantity you please, and make it more than blood-warm, and dissolve honey in it till 'tis strong enough to bear an egg, the breadth of a shilling ; then boil it gently near an hour, taking off the scum as it rises ; then put to about nine or ten gallons seven or eight large blades of mace, three nutmegs quartered, twenty cloves, three or four sticks of cinnamon, two or three roots of ginger, and a quarter of an ounce of Jamaica pepper ; put these spices into the kettle to the honey and water, a whole lemon, with a sprig of sweet-briar and a sprig of rosemary ; tie the briar and rosemary together, and when they have boiled a little while take them out and throw them away ; but let your liquor stand on the spice in a clean earthen pot till the next day ; then strain it into a vessel that is fit for it ; put the spice in a bag, and hang it in the vessel, stop it, and at three months draw it into bottles. Be sure that 'tis fine when 'tis bottled ; after 'tis bottled six weeks 'tis fit to drink.

Fancy drinking Mead with your soup !

Morat was made of honey flavoured with mulberry juice ; and Pigment—which might be drunk at the Royal Academy banquets—was a sweet and rich liquor evolved from highly-spiced wine flavoured with honey.

Metheglin

was also called Hydromel and Oinomel. " The best Receipt whereof," writes an authority, " that I have observed to be made by them is thus :—

They take rasberries which grow in those parts (*i.e.* Swedeland, Muscovia, Russia, and as far as the Caspian Sea) and put them into fair water for two or three nights (I suppose they bruise them first) that the water may extract their taste and colour. Into this water they put of the purest honey, in proportion about one pound of honey to three or four of water. Then to give it a fermentation they put a tost into it dipp'd in the dregs or grounds of beer, which when it hath set the metheglin at work they take out again, to prevent any ill savour it may give ; if they desire to ferment it long they set it in a warm place ; which when they please to hinder or stop, they remove it into a cool place ; after it hath done fermenting they draw it off the lee for present use ; to add to its excellency they hang in it a little bagg, wherein is cinnamon, grains of paradise, and a few cloves. This may do very well for present drinking. But if you would make your metheglin of the same ingredients, and to be kept (time melior-

ating any sort of drinks) you may preserve your
juice of rasberries at the proper season. And when
you make your metheglin, decoct your honey and
water together, and when it is cold then add your
juice of rasberries which was before prepared to
keep, and purifie your metheglin by the means before
prescrib'd, or ferment it, either by a tost dipp'd in
yest, or by putting a spoonful of yest unto it, to
which you may add the little bagg of spices before
mention'd. Then let it stand about a month to be
thorowly purified, and then bottle it, and preserve
it for use, and it may in time become a curious
drink."

I should think so.

This is what Howell (Clerk to the Privy
Council in 1640) wrote about metheglin :—

The juice of Bees, not Bacchus, here behold,
Which British Bards were wont to quaff of old ;
The berries of the grape with Furies swell,
But in the honeycomb the Graces dwell.

" Neither Sir John Barleycorn or Bacchus had
anything to do with it, but it is the pure juice of
the bee, the laborious bee, and the king of insects ;
the Druids and old British Bards were wont to
take a carouse hereof before they entered into
their speculations. But this drink always carried
a kind of state with it, for it must be attended
with a brown toast ; nor will it admit but of one
good draught, and that in the morning ; if more
it will keep a humming in the head, and so
speak too much of the house it comes from, I
mean the hive."

M'yes. I question the advisability of any sort

of carouse before entering into speculations; more especially if Tattersall's Ring be the scene of your speculations, and you intend getting back your losses.

There is no doubt that metheglin was the favourite drink of the Ancient Britons.

Mead and Braggon, or Braggonet,

do not differ materially from metheglin. Here is the recipe :—

Mix the whites of six eggs with twelve gallons of spring-water ; add twenty pounds of the best virgin honey and the peeling of three lemons ; boil it an hour, and then put into it some rosemary, cloves, mace, and ginger ; when quite cold add a spoonful or two of yeast, tun it, and when it has done working stop it up close. In a few months bottle it off, and deposit in a cool cellar.

If this liquor is properly kept, the taste of the honey will go off, and it will resemble Tokay both in strength and flavour. And the chief objection to this as to other ancient potations, appears to be the intolerable quantity of water, whether "spring" or "fair."

We do not make Birch wine nowadays, although the Birch itself frequently makes small boys whine, after conviction of orchard-robbing, or train-wrecking. But it was a favourite tipple with our ancestors, who during the month of March were wont to cut the ends off the birch-boughs, and let the sap drip into bottles suspended from the boughs. For twopence or threepence a gallon the villagers would catch this sap for their wealthier neighbours, regardless of the feelings, and the cartridges, of the owners of the trees. To every gallon of liquor was added a pound of refined sugar, the mixture being boiled for half an hour or so, then set to cool, with a little yeast added thereto, to make it ferment. The result was then put in barrels, together with a small proportion of powdered mace and cinnamon. A month afterwards it was bottled off, and when drunk was said to be " a most delicate, brisk wine, of a flavour like unto Rhenish."

" The Vertues of the Liquor or Blood of the Birch-tree," says the historian, " have not long been discovered, we being beholding to the Learned Van Helmont for it; who in his *Treatise of the Disease of the Stone* hath very much applauded its Vertues against the effects of the Disease, calling the natural Liquor that flows from the wounded Branches of the Tree, the meer Balsom of the Disease. Ale brewed therewith, as well as the Wine that is made of it, wonderfully operates on the Disease. It is also reputed to be a powerful Curer of the Ptisick."

All the same you will hardly get the *alumni* of Eton and Harrow to love their birch.

" What was

Sack ? "

is a question which has often been asked. It was a common name for a drink in the time of Shakespeare, and Falstaff had a terrible reputation as a sackster. The exact nature of the wine is uncertain, but the name is supposed to be derived

from the Spanish *seco*, and the French *sec*, "dry."
Canary (a sort of white Madeira) was often the
wine meant ; and in old churchwarden's accounts
the word sack frequently occurs, as used as a
communion wine, *i.e.* Madeira and port mixed.
That sack was imported from Spain is certain,
and it was first of all sold, in England, in
apothecaries' shops, as a cordial medicine. The
Excise authorities of the time, if there were any,
were in all probability not quite as busy as at the
present day.

The name Canary was formerly applied to
dry, white wines, which were frequently seasoned
with sugar, cinnamon, nutmeg, roasted apples,
and eggs.

Sack Posset

[Sir Walter Raleigh's Recipe.]

Boil together half a pint of sherry and half a pint
of ale, and add gradually a quart of boiling cream or
milk. Sweeten the mixture well, and flavour with
grated nutmeg. Put into a heated dish, cover, and
stand by the fire for two or three hours.

And if you can see the double ox-fences in
Northamptonshire next morning, there is not
much the matter with your liver.

Here is the method of manufacturing

English Sack,

which must be a poor, ill-favoured sort of drink.
It was also known as Saragossa wine.

To every quart of water put a sprig of rue, and
to every gallon a handful of fennel-roots, boil these

half an hour, then strain it out, and to every gallon of this liquor—ugh—put three pounds of honey ; boil it two hours, and scum it well, and when 'tis cold pour it off and tun it into a vessel, or such cask as is fit for it ; keep it a year in the vessel, and then bottle it. 'Tis a very good sack.

And the butler who would place this on my table would get a good sack, too.   Mustard-and-water is cheaper and swifter.

Canary and Rhenish were also drunk freely during the Elizabethan period — the English Sack recipe belongs to the Charles I. period—and long before that usquebaugh, or whisky in all its original sin, was in demand, although the Highlanders were no dabs at distillation until the sixteenth century.   Usquebaugh, by the way, is derived from the old Gaelic *Uisge-beatha*, "Water of Life," and under this name both Irish and Scotch whisky were originally known.

But this simple water of life was not tasty enough for some palates, therefore vile men invented a special blend for the benefit of the wealthy, and those who had not much work to do next morning.

To make Usquebaugh.

To three gallons of brandy put four ounces of aniseeds bruised ; the next day distil it in a cold still pasted up ; then scrape four ounces of licorice, and pound it in a mortar, dry it in an iron pan, do not burn it, put it in the bottle to your distill'd water, and let it stand ten days.   Then take out the licorice, and to every six quarts of the spirits put in cloves, mace, nutmeg, cinnamon and ginger, of each a quarter of an ounce, dates stoned and sliced four ounces; raisins stoned half a pound. Let these infuse ten days, then strain it out, and tincture it with saffron, and bottle it and cork it well.

It seems just the sort for Jubilee rejoicings and vestry meetings; but do not give it to the constable on fixed point duty.

In my pitiable ignorance, I once thought that Clary was the old English name for Claret. Not a bit of it. This is how the artistic used to make

Clary Wine.

Take twenty-four pounds of Malaga raisins, pick and chop them very small, put them in a tub, and to each pound a quart of water; let them steep ten or eleven days—this sounds like a school treat— stirring it twice every day; you must keep it covered close all the while; then strain it off, and put it into a vessel, and about half a peck of the tops of clary (what was clary?) when 'tis in blossom; stop it close for six weeks, and then bottle it off; in two or three months 'tis fit to drink.

Clary naturally leads to

Apricock Wine,

which we of the nineteenth century miscall apricot. The derivation of the word is Latin. Then the Arabs got hold of it, and it became Al-precoc. Then the thriving Spaniards got hold of the word, which became Alborcoque; and so to England. But to the wine.

Take three pounds of sugar, and three quarts of water, let them boil together, and scum it well; then put in six pounds of apricocks, pared and stoned, and let them boil till they are tender; then take them up, and when the liquor is cold bottle it up. You may, if you please, after you have taken out the apricocks, let the liquor have one boil with a sprig of flower'd clary in it.

Also, you may if you please — and you probably *will* please—add a little old brandy to the decoction.

CHAPTER IV

SOME OLD RECIPES

Indifference of the Chineses—A nasty potion—A nastier—White
Bastard—Helping it to be eager—Improving Malmsey—
Death of the Duke of Clarence—Mum is *not* the word—
English champagne—Life without Ebulum a blank—Cock
ale—How to dispose of surplus poultry—Painful fate of a
pauper—*Potage pauvre*—Duties of the old English housewife
—Election of wines, not golf—Muskadine—Lemon wine—
Familiar recipe—King William's posset—Pope's ditto.

"The Chineses," says a very old work on liquid
nourishment, "make excellent Drink of Rice,
which is very pleasant of taste, and is preferred
by them before wine."

But, like the Germans, the Chineses will eat
and drink pretty nearly anything. And this is
the cheering mixture which the Chineses sampled
in the new German colony of Kiant-schan,
according to the *Frankfurter Zeitung* :—

"Sitting under the poplars one can imagine
oneself in the courtyard of an old German feudal
castle. The hamper is opened, and the cold
mountain stream flowing before the temple serves
as an ice cellar. Once more the male population
of the village puts in an appearance, standing

round the table in amazement at all the unheard-of things happening. The greatest success attends the uncorking of the Apollinaris bottles. The bottle is pointed at the onlookers, and the cork having been loosened it flies into their faces with a loud report. At first they are greatly alarmed, then they enjoy the joke hugely, and at last they all squat on the ground in a circle, and send a deputy to the table of the foreigners, bearing a teacup. The petition is granted, and in the teacup an exquisite brew is prepared. The drainings of all the beer bottles are collected, to which is added a little claret and a liberal proportion of Apollinaris, and then, in order to lend greater consistency to the beverage, some sausage skins are mixed with it. The teacup circulates amongst the Chinese, and each sips it with reverential awe. Some of them make fearful grimaces, but not one has the courage of his opinion, and it is evident that, on the whole, the drink is voted a good one, although, perhaps, its flavour is somewhat rare."

Next, please. Oh, here is another, about some neighbours of the Chineses.

"In the Isle Formosa, not far from China, the Natives make a Drink as strong and intoxicative as Sack, out of Rice, which they soak in warm water, and then beat it to a paste in a Mortar ; then they chew some Rice-meal in their mouths, which they spit to a pot till they have got about a quart of liquor, which they put to the paste instead of Leaven or Ferment. And after all be kneaded together till it be Dough, they put it into a great earthen pot, which they

fill up with water, and so let it remain for two
months ; by which means they make one of the
most pleasant Liquors a man need drink ; the
older the better and sweeter, although you keep
it five and twenty or thirty years."

Weel—I hae ma doots.

Until reading " *The English Housewife*, containing the inward and outward Vertues which
ought to be in a complete Woman, published by
Nicholas Okes at the sign of the golden Unicorne,
in 1631," I had no skill in making

White Bastard

or " aparelling " Muskadine.   They used a lot of
eggs in the vintry in those days, and these were
the instructions for making white bastard.

Draw out of a pipe of bastard ten gallans, and
put to it five gallans of new milke, and skim it as
before, and all to beat it with a parill of eight whites
of egges, and a handfull of Baysalt and a pint of
conduit-water, and it will be white and fine in the
morning.   But if you will make very fine bastard—
which I, personally, have no ambition to do—take
a white-wine hog's-head, and put out the lees, and
wash it cleane, and fill it halfe full and halfe a quarter,
and put to it foure gallans of new milke, and beate it
well with the whites of sixe egges, and fill it up with
white-wine and sacke, and it will be white and fine.

Bastard had not much rest in the seventeenth
century.   The housewife who might wish " to
helpe bastard being eager " had to follow these
directions :—

Take two gallons of the best stoned honey, and

two gallons of white wine, and boyle them in a faire panne, skimme it cleane, and straine it through a faire cloth that there be no moats in it ; then put to it one ounce of collianders (coriander seeds ?) and one ounce of aniseeds, foure or five orange pils (pips ?) dry and beaten to powder, let them lye three dayes ; then draw your bastard into a cleane pipe, then put in your honey with the rest, and beate it well ; then let it lye a weeke and touch it not, after draw it at pleasure.

In the present enlightened century such a recipe does not read like helping the possible consumer to be " eager."

Nor does the following method of treating Malmsey sound promising, except for making its consumer particularly " for'ard " :—

If you have a good but of Malmsey, and a but or two of sacke that will not be drunke ; for the sacke prepare some empty but or pipe, and draw it more than halfe full of sacke ; then fill it up with Malmsey, and when your but is full within a little, put into it three gallons of Spanish cute, the best that you can get—where did they get it ? — then beate it well ; then take your taster, and see that it bee deepe coloured ; then fill it up with sacke, and give it aparell, and beate it well. The aparell is thus : Take the yelkes of tenne egges and beate them in a cleane bason with a handful of Bay salt, and a quarte of conduit-water, and beate them together with a little peece of birch, and beate it till it be as short as mosse ; then draw five or sixe gallons out of your but, then beate it againe, and then fill it up, and the next day it will be ready to be drawne. This aparell will serve both for muscadine, bastard, and for sacke.

We are not told in history if the butt of
Malmsey in which the Duke of Clarence shuffled
off his mortal and sinful coil had been previously
subjected to this "aparell" and castigation.   In
the interests of mercy, let us hope not.

The fluid once known as

Mum

never claimed any sort of relationship with
sparkling wine, but was a species of unsophisticated ale, brewed from wheat, or oats, with a
little bean-meal occasionally introduced ; in fact,
the sort of stuff we use in the present century to
fatten bacon pigs upon.   And "mum" has *not* been
the word with British brewers for some time past.

Champagne has been made in England for a
considerable period ; but since the closing of the
"night - houses " in Panton Street the trade
therein has not been very brisk.   During the
present century champagne in this country—and
I grieve to add in France as well—has been
chiefly fabricated from apples, and other fruits ;
but here is a much older way of making

English Champagne.

Take to three gallons of water nine pounds of
Lisbon sugar ; boil the water and sugar half an hour,
scum it clean, then have one gallon of currants
pick'd, but not bruis'd, pour the liquor boiling hot
over them, and when cold work it with half a pint
of balm two days ; then pour it through a flannel
or sieve, then put it into a barrel fit for it with half
an ounce of ising-glass well bruis'd.   When it has
done working stop it close for a month, then bottle

it, and in every bottle put a very small lump of
double-refin'd sugar. This is excellent wine, and
has a beautiful colour.

"Life without Ebulum," writes a friend, an
instructor of youth in the ingenuous arts, in
forwarding me the recipe, "is a void to most
people who have not cultivated the eringo root
in their back gardens." I have never tasted
ebulum, preferring my ale neat and unadorned,
but this is how to prepare

Ebulum.

To a hogshead of strong ale take a heap'd bushel
of elderberries, and half a pound of juniper berries
beaten ; put in all the berries when you put in the
hops, and let them boil together till the berries
break in pieces ; then work it up as you do ale.
When it has done working, add to it half a pound
of ginger, half an ounce of cloves, as much mace,
an ounce of nutmegs, and as much cinnamon grosly
beaten, half a pound of citron, as much eringo root,
and likewise of candied orange-peel. Let the sweet-
meats be cut in pieces very thin, and put with the
spice into a bag, and hang it in the vessel when you
stop it up. So let it stand till 'tis fine, then bottle
it up, and drink it with lumps of double-refin'd
sugar in the glass.

One of the quaintest beverages of which I
ever heard, or read, is

Cock Ale.

In order to make this, the *Compleat Housewyfe*
instructs us to take ten gallons of ale, and a large

cock, the older the better. Parboil the cock, flea
(flay ?) him, and stamp him in a stone mortar till his
bones are broken (you must craw and gut him when
you flea him), then put the cock into two quarts of
sack, and put to it three pounds of raisins of the sun
stoned, some blades of mace, and a few cloves ; put
all these into a canvas bag, and a little before you
find the ale has done working, put the ale and bag
together into a vessel ; in a week or nine days bottle
it up, fill the bottles but just above the neck, and
give it the same time to ripen as other ale.

I have frequently read of the giving of "body"
to ale and stout, by means of the introduction of
horseflesh ; and an old song used to tell us that
upon one of the paupers in a certain workhouse
happening, inadvertently, to fall head-foremost
into the copper,

dreadful to tell, he was boiled in the soup,

which, on that account, in all probability so
strengthened the constitutions of the other
paupers as to render them impatient of workhouse discipline. The man who disappeared
mysteriously—this is Mr. Samuel Weller's story
—and who unwittingly furnished "body" for
the sausages supplied to the neighbourhood, was,
after all, benefiting his fellow-men. But to put
the rooster into the ale-cask smacks somewhat
of barbarism ; and thank goodness we do not
work off our surplus poultry in that fashion
nowadays. But these barbarians were not
ashamed ; for lo ! facing me is "another way"
for the manufacture of rooster-beer.

Take an old red, or other cock, and boyle him

indifferent well ; then flea his skin clean off, and
beat him flesh and bones in a stone mortar all to
mash, then slice into him half a pound of dates, two
nutmegs quartered, two or three blaids of mace,
four cloves ; and put to all this two quarts of sack
that is very good ; stop all this up very close that
no air may get to it for the space of sixteen hours ;
then tun eight gallons of strong ale into your barrel
so timely as it may have done working at the sixteen
hours' end ; and then put thereinto your infusion
and stop it close for five days, then bottle it in
stone bottles ; be sure your corks are very good, and
tye them with pack-thread ; and about a fortnight
or three weeks after you may begin to drink of it ;
you must also put into your infusion two pound of
raisins of the sun stoned.

Holy Moses ! What a drink !
" It is necessary," wrote a chronicler of the
day, "that our English Housewife be skilfull in
the election, preservation, and curing of all sorts
of wines, because they be usuall charges under
her hands, and by the least neglect must turne
the Husband to much losse."

This was written, I may interpolate, before
the bicycle craze had set in, and before the era
of ladies' clubs. Fancy asking the New Woman
to elect, preserve, and cure all sorts of wines !

"Therefore," continues the same writer, "to
speak first of the election of sweete Wines she
must be careful that her Malmseys be full Wines,
pleasant, well hewed, and fine ; that Bastard be
fat, and if it be tawny it skils not, for the tawny
Bastards be always the sweetest. Muskadine
must be great, pleasant, and strong, with a swete

sent, and Amber colour. Sacke, if it be Seres
(Xerez ?), which it should be, you shall know it
by the marke of a corke burned on one side of
the bung, and they be ever full gadge, and so are
no other Sackes ; and the longer they lye the
better they be."

Muskadine

was, apparently, made from bastard and malmsey,
with the addition of ginger and new milk (with
the cream removed).

Here is a potion bearing the harmless, Band-
of-Hopish name of

Lemon Wine,

which would not, however, be tolerated at a
Salvation Army banquet. The first part of the
recipe will be familiar to many of my young
friends.

Take six large lemons, pare off the rind, and cut
the lemons and squeeze out the juice, and in the
juice steep the rind, and put it to a quart of brandy
—so far, brother, the court is with you—and let it
stand in an earthen pot close stop't three days, and
then squeeze six more, and mix with two quarts of
spring-water, and as much sugar as will sweeten the
whole, and boil the water and lemons and sugar
together, and let it stand till 'tis cool. Then add
a quart of white wine and the other lemon and
brandy, and mix them together, and run it through
a flannel bag into some vessel. Let it stand three
months and bottle it off. Cork your bottles very
well, and keep it cool ; it will be fit to drink in a
month or six weeks.

Cheer-oh! This potion reads well, and I know a punch which bears some resemblance thereto. But why call it lemon wine? Do not the brandy and the white wine deserve some recognition in the nomenclature?

What is understood by the name

Barley Wine

nowadays is a particularly strong brew of ale. With the ancients, however, it was a drink which might have been with safety handed round at breaking-up parties in a young ladies' school.

Take half a pound of French barley, and boil it in three waters, and save three pints of the last water, and mix it with a quart of white wine, half a pint of borage-water, as much clary-water, and a little red rose-water, the juice of five or six lemons, three quarters of a pound of fine sugar, and the thin yellow rind of a lemon; brew all these quick together, run it through a strainer, and bottle it up. 'Tis pleasant in hot weather, and very good in fevers.

In the matter of possets — of which more anon — the following reads like a seductive winter's beverage, especially if the imbiber have a cold in the head. Fear not the bile, but read the directions for making

King William's Posset.

Take a quart of cream, and mix with it a pint of ale, then beat the yolks of ten eggs and the whites of four; when they are well beaten, put them to your cream and ale. Sweeten to your taste and slice some nutmeg in it ; set it over the fire, and keep it stirring all the while, and when 'tis thick, and before it boils, take it off, and pour it into the bason you serve it in to the table.

Here is another, even more seductive.

To make the Pope's Posset.

Blanch and beat three-quarters of a pound of almonds so fine that they will spread between your fingers like butter, put in water as you beat them to keep them from oiling. Then take a pint of sack or sherry, and sweeten it very well in double-refin'd sugar, make it boiling hot, and at the same time put half a pint of water to your almonds, and make them boil ; then take both off .the fire, and mix them very well together with a spoon. Serve it in a china dish.

Frontiniac Wine

was simplicity itself.

Take six gallons of water and twelve pounds of white sugar, and six pounds of raisins of the sun cut small ; boil them together one hour ; then take of the flowers of elder, when they are falling and will shake off, the quantity of half a peck ; put them in the liquor when 'tis almost cold, and next day put in six spoonfuls of syrup of lemons, and four spoonfuls of ale yeast ; and two days after put it into a vessel that is fit for it, and when it has stood two months bottle it off.

In the olden times, just before Oliver Cromwell was a going concern, there were two sorts of what was then called

Renish Wine,

that is to say, Elstertune and Barabant.

" The Elstertune," says my informant, "are best, you shall know it by the Fat, for it is double bard and double pinned "—I have not the faintest idea what he means, but those are his words ; " the Barabant is nothing so good, and there is not so much good to be done with them as with the other. If the Wines be good and pleasant, a man may rid away a Hogshead or two of White wine, and this is the most vantage a man can have by them ; and if it be slender and hard, then take three or four gallons of stone-honey and clarify it cleane ; then put into the honey four or five gallons of the same wine, and then let it seeth a great while, and put into it two-pence in cloves bruised, let them seeth together, for it will take away the sent of honey ; and when it is sodden take it off, and set it by till it be thorow cold ; then take foure gallons of milke and order it as before, and then put all into your wine, and all to beate it ; and (if you can) role it, for that is the best way ; then stop it close and let it lie, and that will make it pleasant."

Possibly, but it seems a deal of trouble to take over a wine.

And now let us adjourn to a more familiar subject, for discussion in the next chapter.

CHAPTER V

GLORIOUS BEER

Nectar on Olympus—Beer and the Bible—"Ninepenny" at
Eton—"Number One" Bass—"The wicked weed called
hops"—All is not beer that's bitter—Pathetic story of
"Poor Richard"—Secrets of brewing—Gervase Markham
—An "espen" full of hops—Eggs in ale—Beer soup—The
wassail bowl—Sir Watkin Wynne—Brown Betty—Rum-
fustian—Mother-in-law—A delightful summer drink—
Brasenose ale.

As much poetry has been written in praise of
John Barleycorn as in praise of wine, woman,
battles, heroes, Cupid's darts, and patent medicines. And one dear old song, which seems to
ring in my ears as I write, proclaimed that in
the opinion of the author the nectar which the
gods imbibed from golden goblets on the top of
Mount Olympus was in reality cool, refreshing
pale ale, quaffed out of pewter tankards.
Whether this was so matters not, but as to
the antiquity of beer as a beverage there can be
no question; and however much the demand
for other liquors may have slackened during the
rolling on of time, John Barleycorn is still growing in public estimation. Breweries keep on

springing up all over the country, and those who
purchase shares in them receive, for the most
part, substantial dividends. "Beer and the
Bible" have won more elections than any other
combination ; the organization of the brewers
has hitherto proved powerful enough to withstand
all the slings and arrows of the Prohibition party,
whilst there has been an enormous increase in
the value of houses licensed to sell fermented
refreshment ; and the name of Bass will "live
on," like Claudian, "through the centuries."

There be more than one description of beer
put before the public. I forget at this moment
who was responsible for the "swipes" of my
school days, which tasted like red ink—and I have
sampled both—but I have always believed that
the manufacturer—I do not believe him to have
been a brewer at all—had a special spite against
the rising generation, which he wished to die a
lingering death. The "ninepenny" quaffed
beneath the holy shade of Henry was good,
sound, wholesome tipple ; but I fancy an inferior
brand was poured forth to us at "half time" in
the football field. Since those days I have tasted
pretty nearly all sorts and conditions of beer,
from the "Number One" Bass drawn from the
wood in pewter pots, in a little hostelry just off
the Waterloo Road—the very best according to
my taste—to the awful stuff tasted, and only
tasted, one Sunday in a charmingly rural-looking
little inn, with a thatched roof—a licensed house
which apparently laid itself out to entrap the
daring and enterprising "*bona fide* traveller," and
whose malt liquor was apparently composed for

E

the most part of vinegar and dirty water, in
which had been soaked quassia chips, salt, bloater-
heads, and some of the thatch from the roof.

Beer was the current name in England for
every description of malt liquor before the
introduction of " the wicked weed called hops "
from the Netherlands in 1524. According to
the *Alvismal*, a didactic Scandinavian poem of
the tenth century, this malt liquor was called ale
amongst men, and beer by the gods ; and it was
probably from this Scandinavian poem that the
author of the anything-but-didactic poem quoted
above got his ideas as to the real nature of the
beverage partaken of on Olympus. In the
Eastern counties of England, and over the greater
part of the kingdom, ale signifies strong, and beer
small, malt liquor, but in the West these names
mean exactly the reverse—which must be con-
fusing in the extreme to the intelligent foreigner
on his travels in search of facts and—refreshment.
As now used, ale is distinguished from beer—I
am alluding to the more civilized parts of our
country — chiefly by its strength, and by the
quantity of sugar remaining in it undecomposed.
Strong ale is made from the best pale malt, and
the fermentation is allowed to proceed slowly,
and the ferment to be exhausted and separated.
This, together with the large quantity of sugar
still left undecomposed, enables the liquor to
keep long, without requiring a large amount of
hops.

The last few lines may give the reader the
impression that the writer served his time in
Burton-on-Trent ; but this is not the case. I

have conveyed the bulk of my technical know-ledge of brewing from standard works on the subject.

It will be gathered from some previous remarks that all is not beer that's bitter ; and although it would seem impossible to find a cleaner, healthier, or more strengthening drink than the " pure beer " of commerce, brewed from good English or Scotch barley, Kentish hops, and fair spring-water, how about the wash sold in some licensed houses which is "fetched up" with foot-sugar, bittered with quassia, and mixed with salt and any nasty flavourer which is handy ?

The old stories about the carcass of a horse placed in the London stout, to give it " body," and the mysterious disappearance of an Italian organ-grinder, together with his monkey and infernal machine, just outside a high-class brewery, are probably apocryphal. And although the ancients undoubtedly put a red cock—the older the better —into ale, on occasion, the nineteenth century Briton, for the most part, if the rooster be too tough to serve as a boiled *bonne bouche* with parsley-and-butter, usually makes Cock-a-Leekie of him. And thereby hangs a tale.

When my firm was running a small chicken-ranche we once reared an unfortunate fowl, who had curvature of the spine, almost from the fracture of his shell. He was a weakling, and his brethren and sistren, after the manner of birds, beasts, and fishes, who " go for " the anæmic and infirm, persecuted him exceedingly, and pecked most of his feathers off. Being a

merciful, and withal a thrifty, poultry-farmer, I
looked out an old parrot's cage from the tool-shed,
and in this cage installed the weakly cockerel.
He was forthwith christened "Poor Richard,"
and given little Benjamin's share of the corn and
wine, and cayenne pepper and—other things.
And although his head was still slewed round to
starboard, he thrived under his liberal nourishment
and freedom from the assaults of his relatives.

Time flew on. I had been the "Northern
Circuit," in the pursuit of my then profession of
reporter of the sport of kings. I returned home
late on a Saturday night, and next day we had
friends to dinner. So much North Country
language, and so much travelling about had quite
put our feathered and afflicted pensioner out of
my head ; and even the fact of our having the
favourite broth of His Majesty King James the
First for dinner did not suggest anything to my
busy brain. But afterwards, when we were
alone—she ought not to have done it—my life-
partner confided to me that I had helped to eat
"Poor Richard"! And I felt like a very
cannibal ; and mourned the bird as a brother.

But to return. In Queen Elizabeth's reign
it was, I used to believe, a capital offence to put
hops into beer. But these are the directions for

Brewing of Strong Ale,

issued by one Gervase Markham, an authority on
the subject, and a contemporary of Shakespeare ;
and in these directions "hops" are distinctly
mentioned as one of the component parts of the
brew.

Now for the brewing of strong Ale, because it is drinke of no such long lasting as Beere is, therefore you shall brew lesse quantity at a time thereof, as two bushels of Northerne measure (which is foure bushels or halfe a quarter in the South) at a brewing, and not above, which will make foureteene gallons of the best Ale. Now for the mashing and ordering of it in the mash-fat, it will not differ any thing from that of Beere ; as for hops, although some use not to put in any, yet the best Brewers thereof will allow to foureteene gallons of Ale a good espen full of hops, and no more, yet before you put in your hops, as soone as you take it from the graines, you shall put it into a vessell, and change it, or blinke it in this manner : Put into the Wort a handfull of Oke-bowes and a pewter dish, and let them lye therein till the Wort looke a little paler than it did at the first, and then presently take out the dish and the leafe, and then boile it a full houre with the hops, as aforesayd, and then clense it, and set it in vessels to cook ; when it is milk-warme, having set your Barme to rise with some sweete Wort ; then put all into the guilfat, and as soone as it riseth, with a dishe or bowle beate it in, and so keepe it with continuall beating a day and a night, and after run it. From this Ale you may also draw halfe so much very good middle Ale, and a third part very good small Ale.

Another way

To make Strong Beer

was published at a later date than the above, and to my thinking is not a better way.

To a barrel of beer take two bushels of malt and half a bushel of wheat just crackt in the mill, and some of the flour lifted out of it ; when your water is scalding hot, put it in your mashing-fat; there let it stand till you can see your face in it ; then put your malt upon it, then put your wheat upon that, and do not stir it ; let it stand two hours and a half ; then let it run into a tub that has two pounds of hops in it, and a handful of rosemary flowers, and when 'tis all run put it in your copper and boil it two hours ; then strain it off, setting it a-cooling very thin, and set it a-working very cool ; clear it very well before you put it a-working, put a little yeast to it ; when the yeast begins to fall, put it into your vessel, and when it has done working in the vessel, put in a pint of whole wheat and six eggs ; then stop it up, let it stand a year, and then bottle it. Then mash again, stir the malt very well in, and let it stand two hours, and let that run, and mash again, and stir it as before ; be sure you cover your mashing-fat well up, mix the first and second running together ; it will make good household beer.

I rather fancy the blending of a lot of eggs (presumably new-laid) with the mash, would " break " some of the smaller brewers. It could hardly be done at the price.

The Germans make

Beer Soup.

Whether this is made from British or lager beer is not stated in the recipe before me, which hardly reads suited to the ordinary English palate.

I will now give a few modern recipes for tasty beer-compounds.

Ale Cup (Cold).

Squeeze the juice of a lemon into a round of hot toast ; lay on it a thin piece of the rind, a tablespoonful of powdered sugar, a little grated nutmeg or powdered all-spice, and a sprig of balm. Pour over these one wine-glass of brandy, two of sherry, and three pints of mild ale. Do not allow the balm to remain in many minutes.

Ale Flip (Hot).

Put into a saucepan three pints of ale, a tablespoonful of sugar, a blade of mace, a clove, and a small piece of butter, and bring the liquor to a boil. Beat the white of one egg and the yolks of two thoroughly, mixing with them a tablespoonful of cold ale. Mix all together, and then pour the whole rapidly from one large jug to another, from a good height—mind your fingers and the furniture—for some minutes, to froth it thoroughly. Do not allow it to get cool.

Ale Posset (Hot).

Boil a pint of new milk, and pour it over a slice of toasted bread. Stir in the beaten yolk of an egg and a small piece of butter, and sugar *ad lib*. Mix these with a pint of hot ale, and boil for a few minutes. When the scum rises the mixture is ready for use.

Mulled Ale (Very Hot).

Put half a pint of ale, a clove, a little whole ginger, a piece of butter the size of a marble, and a teaspoonful of sugar into a saucepan, and bring

it to boiling-point. Beat two eggs with a tablespoonful of cold ale, and pour the boiling ale into
them, and then into a large jug. Pass the whole from
one jug to another, as in the case of Ale Flip, return
to saucepan, and heat it again till almost, *not quite*,
at boiling-point.

With regard to

Wassail, or Swig (Cold),

which used to be a very popular beverage at the
universities—at one time it was peculiar to Jesus
College, Oxford—is of very ancient date indeed.

"Sir quod he," is part of a conversation culled
from an old MS., "Watsayll, for never days of
your lyf ne dronk ye of such a cuppe," which
sounds as if the Watsayll was of a seductive and
harmful nature. Nevertheless here is the recipe,
taken from "Oxford Nightcaps."

Put into a bowl half a pound of Lisbon sugar (if
you do not possess that brand, I have no doubt
"best lump," pulverized, will do as well), and pour
on it one pint of warm beer ; grate a nutmeg and
some ginger into it ; add four glasses of sherry and
five additional pints of beer ; stir it well and
sweeten to taste ; let it stand covered up two or
three hours, then put three or four slices of bread
cut thin and toasted brown into it, and it is fit for
use. Sometimes two or three slices of lemon are
introduced, together with a few lumps of sugar
rubbed on the peel of a lemon. Bottle this mixture,
and in a few days it may be drunk in a state of
effervescence.

On the festival of St. David, an immense silver-
gilt bowl, the gift of Sir Watkin W. Wynne to

the college in 1732 is filled with this "swig," and passed round, at Jesus College. And I should prefer to call the beverage "swig" instead of "wassail," which should properly be a *hot* drink, if we are to believe the illustrated papers at Christmas-time. And there is no toast in the orthodox Wassail, but, instead, roasted apples. What does Puck say in *A Midsummer Night's Dream?*

> Sometime lurk I in a gossip's bowl,
> In very likeness of a roasted crab,
> And when she drinks against her lips I bob,
> And on her wither'd dewlaps pour the ale.

Brown Betty

Here is another old recipe :—

Dissolve a quarter of a pound of brown sugar in one pint of water, slice a lemon into it, let it stand a quarter of an hour, then add a small quantity of pulverised cloves and cinnamon, half a pint of brandy, and one quart of good strong ale ; stir it well together, put a couple of slices of toasted bread in it, grate some nutmeg and ginger over the toast, and it is fit for use. Ice it well, and it will prove a good summer, warm it and it will become a pleasant winter, beverage. It is drunk chiefly at dinner.

Rather heavily loaded for a dinner drink, I should say.

Another recipe for

Ale Flip

will serve, here.

Beat well together in a jug, four eggs with a
quarter of a pound of sifted sugar ; then add by
degrees, stirring all the time, two quarts of old Burton
ale, and half a pint of gin ; pour backwards and for-
wards from one jug to another, and when well frothed
serve in tumblers.   Grate a little nutmeg atop of each
portion.   This is one of the best "nightcaps" I
know—especially after you may have been badger-
hunting, or burgling, or serenading anybody on
Christmas Eve.

Rumfustian.

Beat up in a jug, the yolks of two eggs with a
tablespoonful of sifted sugar ; then take half a pint
of old Burton ale, one wine-glass of gin, one wine-
glass of sherry, a little spice and lemon rind.   Let
the ale, wine, and gin, mixed together come to the
boil, then pour in the egg mixture, whisking rapidly ;
serve hot, with a little nutmeg grated atop.

Such compound drinks, into which ale enters,
as Shandy-gaff require no mention here.   Suffice
it to mention that this gaff has for many years
been the favourite beverage of those who go up
the river—there is but one river in England—in
boats, whether schoolboys, or of riper years.
In Stock Exchange circles champagne is occasionally substituted for ginger-beer, but this is
a combination in which I have no implicit belief ;
although champagne and Guinness's stout make
an excellent mixture.   Stout and bitter, otherwise known as

Mother-in-law,

and old-and-mild, for which the pet name is

Uncle,

are also in much request amongst the ground-
lings ; whilst during the warm weather I know
of no more popular swallow, for moderate drinkers,
who do not require their throats to be scratched,
than a small bottle of lemonade to which is
added just one " pull " of pale-ale. This is called,
for the sake of brevity, a

Small Lem and a Dash,

or the Poor Man's Champagne ; and is a refreshing and innocuous drink which might commend
itself to total abstainers.

In the Universities of Oxford and Cambridge
there is probably as much malt liquor drunk per
head as in any other part of the world.

Brasenose Ale

has obtained a reputation which the beverage
doubtless fully merits. Since the foundation of
this college a custom has prevailed of introducing
into the refectory on Shrove Tuesday, immediately after dinner, what is denominated
Brasenose Ale, but what is known in many
other parts of England as Lamb's Wool. Verses
in praise of the Ale are—or at all events were
—annually written by one of the undergraduates,
and a copy of them is sent to every resident
member of the College.

The following stanzas are taken from one of
these contributions :—

Shall all our singing now be o'er,
  Since Christmas carols fail ?
No ! Let us shout one stanza more
  In praise of Brasenose Ale !

A fig for Horace and his juice,
  Falernian and Massic ;
Far better drink can we produce,
  Though 'tis not quite so classic.

Not all the liquors Rome e'er had
  Can beat our matchless Beer ;
Apicius' self had gone stark mad
  To taste such noble cheer.

After all, the potion is simplicity itself :—

Three quarts of ale, sweetened with sifted sugar,
and served up in a bowl with six roasted apples floating in it.

CHAPTER VI

ALL ALE

Waste not, want not—The right hand for the froth—Arthur
Roberts and Phyllis Broughton—A landlord's perquisites—
Marc Antony and hot coppers—Introduction of ale into
Britain — Burton-on-Trent — Formerly a cotton-spinning
centre—A few statistics—Michael Thomas Bass—A grand
old man—Malting barleys—Porter and stout—Lager beer—
Origin of bottled ale—An ancient recipe—Lead-poisoning—
The poor man's beer.

In a speech made some years ago Sir Michael
Hicks-Beach observed that nearly one million
sterling's worth of tobacco was wasted annually
by throwing away cigarette-ends and the stumps
of cigars. But what would you, Sir Michael?
Are the lieges to cremate their lips and singe
their moustaches by smoking on to the (literally)
bitter end? Whether or no, it is tolerably certain that there is an enormous daily waste in
the matter of intoxicating drinks — without
counting the wanton, although conscientious,
destruction made by teetotal magnates. According to statistics—I shall not madden my readers
with many of these—more than £138,000,000

are spent annually in Great Britain on spirituous
liquors. Half of this sum, it may be fairly stated,
is spent in the provinces. It may also be taken
as read that 5 per cent of beer and stout is
wasted, in the way of froth, spillings, and leav-
ings, and 3 per cent of spirits. This brings us
face to face with the calculation that the value
of our daily waste in drinks is nearly £6500.
Carbonic acid gas is undoubtedly answerable
for a lot of this waste. In *The Old Guard*,
a musical piece produced at the Avenue
Theatre some years ago, Mr. Arthur Roberts in
his instructions to Miss Phyllis Broughton—
who made a very comely stage barmaid—particularly enjoined her, when drawing ale, to use
her left hand to bring the handle down.

"The right hand," he observed—of course it
was all "gag"—"is for the froth." And then
he shewed her how to make half a pint of liquor
fill a pint measure. Of course there be some
professional imbibers who would object strongly
and refuse to accept the froth programme ; but
on the other hand it pays the retailer, in the long-
run. I am not going to re-tell the old story of
the Quaker ; but will only mention that in the
early seventies the landlord of a favourite tavern
in the Strand—a house of call for histrions, which
has since then been transmogrified and adorned
with much bevelled glass and carved walnut
—once confided to me that he made every bit of
£300 per annum out of his froth. His barmaids
were all of angelic appearance, with most beautiful
heads of hair (the girls wore plenty of it in those
days) and a wealth of pretty prattle. And the

customers being susceptible, and liberal-minded, the rest was easy.

Egyptian manuscripts written at least 3000 years before the Christian era shew conclusively that even at that primitive period the manufacture of an intoxicating liquor from barley or other grain was extensively carried out in Egypt. Probably the wretched Israelites got far more birch and bastinado than beer given them whilst engaged in brickmaking; but it is quite on the cards that Cleopatra, when fatigued with practising the spot stroke on her billiard-table, often commanded one of her slaves to draw her a pint of bitter with a head on it; and who knows but that her beloved Antony cooled his coppers with small ale?

Pliny—who would be a useful sort of man to have in a daily newspaper office nowadays—records that in his time a fermented drink made from "corn and water" was in regular use in all the districts of Europe with which he was acquainted. But in Britain little was known about beer before the Roman conquest, as the favourite beverages of our ancestors were mead and cider. But the Romans, although they never quite succeeded in subduing the stubborn dispositions of the "barbarians," managed to teach them a bit of husbandry, and to shew them something about brewing. There were no means of making wine in those days, and—save in Wales— there were no grapes to make it with; but the Latins were not long in teaching the Britons— who were never slow to learn anything which might lead to revelry—that a very good sub-

stitute for wine might be expressed from grain
and water. Hops were undoubtedly known
in England before the conquest, but do not
appear to have been regularly used in brewing
before the beginning of the sixteenth century.
It is probable, therefore, that they were employed
as medicine—and there is no better tonic than
your hop. The Germans would seem to have
brewed with the "wicked weed" before the
Englanders did, according to the omniscient
Pliny.

The horny-handed son of toil, who can put
away his four or five gallons daily during harvest-
time, without falling off the waggon, may not
know it, but it is only the female hop which is
used by the brewer of to-day. The characteristics of the he-hop are not known to the
writer, or whether he plays any part in aiding
to relieve the thirst of the lieges; but the
female is said to exercise "a purifying, a pre-
servative, and an aromatic influence over the
wort."

It used to be a popular fallacy that the beer
made at Burton-on-Trent was brewed from
Trent water, instead of, as was and is the case,
from spring-water, which is eminently suited to
the purpose. The chief industry at Burton was,
originally, cotton-spinning, but fifty years ago
this industry was discontinued owing to the
triumphal march of John Barleycorn. Why
spin cotton when the manufacture of beer is not
only a much healthier occupation but is far
more lucrative? So Burton stuck to its beer-
making, a trade which was originally established

there—in a very small way—in the sixteenth century. There appears to have been a demand for Burton ale in London, during the reign of Charles I.; although details are missing as to whether the demand extended to the royal palaces. It is certain, however, that more than one hundred years ago Burton-on-Trent did a considerable export trade with the Baltic. In 1791 there were nine breweries here, and in 1851 sixteen. But at the beginning of the present century, until the last-named year, when the great Exhibition attracted all the world and his wife to England, the breweries at Burton were not all in a flourishing condition; and I have more than once heard my grandfather—who spoke from personal knowledge—tell the story of how the late Mr. Michael Thomas Bass most magnanimously offered to "prop up" another large firm, with the remark, "There's room enough for us both here!"

At present there are thirty breweries in Burton - on - Trent, and employed in these are some 8000 men and boys. After the opening of the Midland Railway in 1839 the brewing trade here began to improve, but it was mainly due to the energy and practical knowledge of Mr.

Bass

aforementioned that Burton-on-Trent in general, and the great firm of Bass are in their present flourishing condition. In the words of Shakespeare, " He was a man ; take him for all in all we shall not look upon his like again." Beginning as traveller to the firm, he was not long ere

F

he became its chief director. He was untiring in business, a man possessing the broadest views of men and things, a bit crotchety on occasion, but possessed of "that most excellent gift of charity," in boundless supplies. Amongst his other benefactions was the building and endowment of St. Paul's, Burton, and the gift of recreation grounds, a free library, and swimming-baths to the adjacent town of Derby. He also built and endowed another church on his own estate, at Rangemore; and his hand was never out of his cash-pocket when he could aid in a good work. He represented Derby, in the Liberal interest, from 1848 to 1883, and was a tower of strength to that party, albeit possessed of nothing like bigoted opinions. On the contrary, it was his custom through life, like Hal o' the Wynd in *The Fair Maid of Perth*, to "fight for his own hand." And as an instance of his energy and grit, it may be mentioned that after voting in the House of Commons for Mr. Gladstone's Irish Church Disestablishment Bill— the division on which did not take place till 2 A.M.—he travelled by the "newspaper train" at 5 A.M. from Euston to Rugeley in order to hunt with Mr. Hugo Meynell Ingram's hounds, later in the morning, changing his clothes on the way down. The meet was at Brereton Hayes, close to Cunnock Chase, and I well remember greeting him that morning, and receiving for a reply : "Thank you, I'm pretty well for an old 'un." He was over seventy (I think) at the time. That was three decades ago ; and since then the trade of Bass has increased enormously.

For the annual holiday of the staff I should be afraid to state from memory how many special trains are required to convey the great hive of workers to Brighton, and other far-distant watering-places, and back to Burton again. In short, it would be hard to find a spot in the inhabited world in which the name of Bass is not known and respected.

I mentioned further back Scotch and English barleys as being employed for malting purposes ; but as a matter of fact the produce of many countries is used, in a blend, the whole being divided into two classes, heavy and light. And in making choice of barleys it is necessary that they should be thoroughly and equally ripened, well "got" or harvested, and as far as possible presented to the brewer in the perfect husk or envelope with which nature has furnished the kernel. Ancient and modern modes of thrashing and dressing to a greater or less extent damage both the husk and the kernel, and thus at the very threshold introduce one of the causes of disease. Whenever the grain is broken or bruised it is liable to be attacked when moist by a variety of moulds which lead to more or less serious disaster.

Of the different varieties of beer, "pale ale" or "bitter" is a highly-hopped beer made from the very finest selected malt and hops ; whilst "mild ale," or as it is called in Scotland "sweet ale," is of greater gravity or strength, and is comparatively lightly hopped. "Old ale" is, naturally, the best stuff that can be brewed, in a state of maturity ; and it is a peculiarity of ale that, securely bottled, it will keep its strength far longer than any other fermented drink.   In December 1889 some bottles of beer were found walled up in a cellar at Burton-on-Trent; and the records of the firm, as well as the shape of the bottles, shewed that the beer had been brewed nearly a hundred years before.   It was as bright as a sunbeam, and quite drinkable, but had lost its bitterness, and assumed the character of sherry. But old ale, like old brandy, is of little value to the toper, in that it takes a very minute quantity to accomplish in him the desired effect—oblivion. " Audit " ales and " college " ditto require very delicate handling of the jug; and I have tasted ancient beer in Allsopp's cellars in Burton, a wine-glassful of which would probably have put a coal-whipper on his back.   It was the colour of mahogany and oh ! so seductive.

Porter, as most people know, is a black beer, brewed in much the same manner as the other stuff, with roasted malt to give it colour ; whilst stout is simply a superior kind of porter.   As for the lager beer of the Fatherland it is fermented at a very low temperature, the fermentation being longer delayed.   Some years ago great stress was laid on the German system of mashing called the " thick mash," which consisted of boiling or cooking a portion of the mash, and running it back and remixing it with the portion left in the tun ; but it is now found possible to brew the finest lager beer with a slight modification of our own mashing method.

The sons of Britannia for a considerable period held aloof from this lager, which was pronounced by some to be mere "hogwash," and by others to consist principally of the juice of fir-cones and onions mixed with snow-water. The fir-cone flavour is, I believe, accounted for by the "pitching" of the barrels in which the beer is stored; but I don't know where the oniony flavour comes from. The prejudice against this beer has long since departed from our midst; in fact it has become quite a favourite summer drink. It is generally considered less intoxicating than its English cousin. In fact the German students are in the habit of putting huge quantities thereof out of sight, on the occasion of passing examinations, and public rejoicings; and these "beer-drinkings" are, apparently, fully sanctioned by the authorities.

It has been written that it is to Dean Nowell, "classed by Fuller among the worthies of England," that we are indebted for the discovery of bottled beer. According to Fuller, "this worthy, who was an enthusiastic fisherman, was one day angling in the Thames; but at the very time when he was trying to catch perch to carry to the frying-pan, that benighted bigot Bishop Bonner was trying to catch him to tie him to the stake for purposes of cremation, to the glory of the old religion. The reverend gentleman heard that he was 'wanted,' left his fishing, and fled as far from the Thames as he could, leaving untasted in a safe place a bottle of beer which he had filled in the morning. Bonner's day did not last long, and Dean Nowell was soon able to return to his old haunts. Fishing as usual, he went to look after his bottle of beer, and

found that it had turned into a species of gun—
it exploded its contents, when touched." Thus
Nature, which is ever kind, turned the martyrdom
and misery of Bloody Mary's reign to good—
it brought about bottled beer. The Dean un-
bosomed himself of his great discovery to his
clerical friends, and the clergy let it out gradually
to the laity.

Gervase Markham, the aforementioned contemporary of Shakespeare, gives the following
directions to "the English Housewife" of 1631,
for

Brewing of Bottle-Ale.

Touching the brewing of Bottle-ale, it differeth
nothing at all from the brewing of strong Ale, onely
it must be drawne in a larger proportion, as at least
twenty gallons of halfe a quarter; and when it
comes to be changed, you shall blinke it (as was
before shewed) more by much than was the strong
Ale, for it must bee pretty and sharpe, which giveth
the life and quicknesse to the Ale : and when you
tunne it, you shall put it into round bottles with
narrow mouthes, and then stopping them close with
corke, set them in a cold sellar up to the wast in
sand, and be sure that the corkes be fast tied in
with strong packe-thrid, for feare of rising out, or
taking vent, which is the utter spoyle of the Ale.

Now for the small drinke arising from this
Bottle-ale, or any other beere or ale whatsoever, if
you keep it after it is blinckt and boyled in a close
vessell, and then put it to barme every morning as
you have occasion to use it, the drinke will drinke
a great deale the fresher, and be much more lively
in taste.

I confess that the above directions are somewhat vague to my untutored mind, which is
quite a blank upon the subject of "blinckt and
boyled" ale. Nor do I imagine for one moment
that the "English Housewife" of the year 1899
will cumber herself with brewing or bottling,
any sort of malt-liquor, as long as there be
bonnets to be chosen, bicycles to be ridden, or
golf to be played.

Wholesome as may be the beer in itself, its
surroundings are not always hygienic. The
system of pumping up the glorious fluid from
the cellar through leaden pipes neither improves
the flavour nor renders it more valuable as a
morning "livener." And there is a story—
which I believe to be strictly true—told of a
night cabman in London who used to call at the
nearest tavern to his stand, the first thing in the
morning, and swallow the first glass of beer
drawn for the day. His end was lead-poisoning.

But there! John Barleycorn has probably
done far more good than harm in his day ; so
let us toast the "Egyptian drink" in itself, the
while we sing, in the words of the old song :—

> Dang his eyes,
> If ever he tries
> To rob a poor man of his beer !

CHAPTER VII

A SPIRITUOUS DISCOURSE

What is brandy?—See that you get it—Potato-spirit from the
Fatherland—The phylloxera and her ravages—Cognac oil—
Natural history of the vine-louse—"Spoofing" the Yanks
—Properties of Argol—Brandy from sawdust—Desiccated
window-sills—Enormous boom in whisky—Dewar and the
trade—Water famine—The serpent Alcohol—Some figures
—France the drunken nation, not Britain — Taxing of
distilleries—*Uisge beatha*—Fusel oil—Rye whisky—Palm
wine—John Exshaw knocked out by John Barleycorn.

"WHAT is a pound?" was a favourite query of
the great Sir Robert Peel. "What is brandy?"
is a question asked now and then; and the
answer thereto should be an ambiguous one.
Brandy is supposed, by good easy people who
trouble not to enquire too closely into the composition of their daily food, to be a liquid
obtained by distilling the fermented juice of the
grape. The red wines are preferable, although
in the seventeenth century the best French
brandy was made entirely from white ones.
The original distillation is clear and colourless,
but when placed in casks the liquid dissolves out
the colouring matter of the wood, brown sugar
and other pigments being also added.

But if you want the best French brandy,
distilled from the luscious grape, see that you
get it; and let your vision be in thorough
working order. With the exception of the
good, conscientious spirit-distillers, all French
houses import potato-spirit in large quantities
from Germany, and re-ship it to the home of
the brave and free as superior cognac. This
alone would seem sufficient excuse for another
invasion of France; although these evil-minded
distillers seek to justify their actions by blam-
ing the *phylloxera*, a little 'insect which has
laboured more assiduously in the cause of
temperance—by destroying the main source of
intemperance—than Sir Wilfrid Lawson himself.
"The ravages of the *phylloxera*," say the distillers,
in effect, "compel us to employ other *matériel*,
in order to fulfil our cognac contracts with the
merchants of the perfidious isle." It is related
of a theatrical "property-man" that, upon
being rebuked by the tragedian for making a
snowstorm out of brown, instead of white, paper,
he replied curtly: "It was the only paper I had;
and if you can't snow white you must snow
brown." This excuse is on a par with that
urged on behalf of the German potato-spirit.

Phylloxera vastatrix (why not *devastatrix?*) has
cost France, it is said, a pecuniary loss far exceed-
ing that of the Franco-Prussian war. The little
monster was discovered in North America in
1854, and whether the discoverer or one of his
friends brought the vine-killer on a holiday-trip
to Europe, or whether it worked its own passage
will never be known. But certain it is that the

little monster made its first appearance on this
side in the year 1863. Striking an attitude,
with the exclamation, " Hallo ! here's a vine,
let's have the first suck," the *phylloxera* commenced a long starring engagement (to borrow
another metaphor from the theatres), which in
another fifteen years' time had developed into
an enormous success, as far as the *vastatrix* was
concerned. Naturally, it is the she-phylly who
does the harm. From August to October Madam
lays her little eggs on the vine-leaves, beneath the
surface. The *ova* develop late in autumn into males
and females, who migrate to the stem of the vine.
There each bold, bad female lays an egg, under
the bark. This egg lies dormant, after the
manner of pesky little insect-nuisances, through
the winter, and develops in April or May into
a wingless, voracious, merciless little "vine-
louse," with power to add to its number. " The
rest," as the mechanical engineers tell us, just
before our brains go, "is easy." The vine-
louse attacks the roots, without waiting, the silly
idiot, for the grapes to ripen, the vine dies, and
the potato reigns in its stead. Without burning
the plant, or drowning it, it is impossible to eradi-
cate the *phylloxera*, without spending three times
as much cash, in chemicals, as the vine is worth.
This is the true story of France's great trouble.

Beetroot-spirit is also largely used in making
cognac, the coarse spirit being flavoured with
œnanthic æther, cognac-oil (made from palm-
oil) and—other things. Also of late years the
French have discovered that almost as good wine
can be made from raisins as from the uncooked

article, provided they use enough raisins ; three pounds being required to make a gallon of liquor. A good deal can also be done, in the way of imitation wine, by chemicals ; it being quite possible to make sherry which will fetch at least four shillings per bottle, for the ridiculous sum of fourpence for the same quantity. And it is also a fact that a large quantity of alleged claret which (mainly through the endeavours of the late Mr. W. E. Gladstone) we are able to import on the cheap from the other side of the water, is made from currants and raisins steeped in water and mixed with cheap Spanish wine.

And what is to be said of British brandy ? A country which can manufacture superior Dorset butter from Thames mud, and real turtle-soup from snails and conger-eels, is not likely to get "left" in a matter of distilling. A great deal of brandy is, therefore, made in the tight little island from ordinary grain alcohol, by adding Argol—I'll tell ye what this is presently —bruised French plums, French wine-vinegar, a little—a very little—good cognac, and redis-tilling. I believe that it is also possible to extract a good midnight sort of brandy—speci-ally recommended for roysterers—from coal-tar and paraffin.

The Americans make brandy from peaches and other stone-fruits, good wholesome liquor, but their French cognac is not to be recom-mended. For it is nothing more nor less than the common whisky which America has exported to France, sent back again, after the necessary treatment. Fact.

Argol, mentioned just now, is a crude variety of cream of tartar which forms a crust within wine-vats and bottles. Originally it exists in the juice of the grape, and is soluble therein; but during the fermentation of the juice, and as it passes into wine, much alcohol is developed, which remaining in the fermenting liquor, causes the precipitation of Argol. Thus the "crust" of port wine is Argol, the principal uses (and abuses) of which are in the preparation of (besides cognac) cream of tartar and tartaric acid. And malicious people say that you have only to scratch French brandy to find the Tartar.

A few years ago a German chemist discovered that a very drinkable brandy can be made from sawdust—whether deal sawdust or any description of dust does not appear; and under the heading, "A New Danger to Teetotalism," an American journal published the following effusion:—

"We are a friend of the temperance movement, and want it to succeed; but what chance can it have when a man can take a rip-saw and go out and get drunk with a fence-rail? What is the use of a prohibitory liquor law if a man is able to make brandy-smashes out of the shingles on his roof, or if he can get delirium tremens by drinking the legs of his kitchen chairs? You may shut up an inebriate out of a gin shop and keep him away from taverns, but if he can become uproarious on boiled sawdust and desiccated window-sills, any effort must necessarily be a failure."

I can believe in the ability of most German chemists to do most things; and possibly sawdust is used in the Fatherland for the manufacture of lager beer, Rhine wine, and—but 'tis a saw subject.

The pure brandy at Cognac is divided into two principal classes—"champagne" brandy, from grapes grown on the plains, and "bois" brandy, the product of wooded districts—I am *not* alluding now to sawdust—and the last-named variety is subdivided into many different names. It takes eight and a half gallons of wine to furnish one gallon of spirits ; and the ravages of the vine-louse have made a terrible difference in the supply. In fact, the amount produced in 1897 was about one-tenth of the amount produced twenty years previously. But thanks to beet-root, potatoes, and—other things, the distiller manages to " get " there just the same. But the man who wrote in 1889, prophesying the speedy disappearance of pure *eau de vie* from the market, was probably not far wrong. " It would seem on the whole," he wrote, " that unless the phylloxera be stamped out, pure brandy will soon be a thing of the past." But they do not tell you this in saloon-bars, and places where they drink.

It was stated by Mr. Dewar last year (1898) that there were 89,000,000 gallons of whisky lying idle in bond because sufficient suitable water to dilute it to the orthodox strength could not be found. This statement is calculated to give a moderate drinker the gapes ; whilst Sir Wilfrid Lawson and others must have longed for permission to set fire to every bonded warehouse in the Kingdom. But the same great authority

on the wines of bonnie Scotland made another
statement at the same time which is eminently
calculated to remove all fears lest whisky, like
brandy, be on the down line. "The serpent
Alcohol," remarks a writer in the *Daily Tele-
graph*, in discussing Mr. Dewar's speech, "may
have been scotched" — was this meant for a
joke ?—" but it is far from having been killed."
According to the Ex-Sheriff's statistics the distillation of Irish whisky, despite its diminishing
popularity, has increased during the last fourteen
years by about thirty per cent ; while in Scotland during the same period the increase has
been at the rate of nearly eighty per cent.
Ireland, that is to say, which produced eleven
million gallons in 1884, now produces fourteen
million and a half gallons ; while the Scotch
output, which was eighteen million gallons in
the former year, had risen in 1898 to the enormous figure of thirty-three millions and a half.
Hech sirs ! these be braw figures indeed.

Yet let not the British be held up to reproba-
tion as hard drinkers, as long as France is a
going concern. Statistics prove that in Scotland,
the land o' the barley bree, the consumption of
spirits during the year 1892-93 averaged a little
more than twelve and a half pints per month,
which is little more than the proportion of spirits
required by the Parisians, without wine, absinthe,
and—other things. The boulevardiers are called
"temperate," although they drink as much spirits
as do the Scots, and thirty times as much wine,
not to mention cider and beer.

Distilling in Britain dates from the eleventh

century, but in the beginning it was worked
solely in the monasteries by the jovial monks.
What a good time those monks of old would
seem to have had ! According to the popular
prints they were usually engaged either in fishing, eating oysters, drinking out of flagons,
catching beetles, confessing pretty women, or
being shaved ; and we know that their abiding-
places were built, for the most part, on the banks
of a river which absolutely swarmed with salmon
or trout, in the midst of a district teeming with
game. Any how the monks made spirits, or
"strong waters" as they were called in those
days, first.

Pure malt whisky is, and has been, made
almost exclusively in Scotland. In Ireland they
use about one-third of malt to two-thirds of oats
and maize. In England they make whisky of
pretty nearly everything, including German spirit,
petroleum, and old boots ; whilst in gallant little
Wales — well the only acknowledged Welsh
whisky I have tasted was excellent in quality,
and apparently made from pure malt. Distilling,
as a trade, commenced in England during the
Tudor period, and from the reputation bluff
King Hal bore for feathering his nest, it is
probable that the industry was fully taxed. In
1579 Scotch distilleries were taxed for the first
time. In Ireland as far back as the eleventh century the natives made *uisge beatha*—now called
potheen—without interference from landlord or
gauger, and continued at it until the sixteenth
century, when licenses were enforced in the cases
of *all but the gentry*, and to run an illicit still was

punishable with death and dismemberment. But
they ran 'em just the same ; for in those days
an Irishman was never really happy unless he
were drinking, fighting, or being sentenced to
death. But whether it was English, Scotch,
Welsh, or Irish whisky, or French brandy, or
Dutch gin, smuggling and illicit distilling were
rampant through the centuries, and the Inland
Revenue officer was no more respected or wor-
shipped than at the present day. Still there has
not been much blood shed over those differences
of opinion ; except in Western Pennsylvania at
the close of the last century—a period when the
greater part of the universe was fighting about
something—when it took 15,000 soldiers from
Washington to quell a riot amongst a populace
discontented with the Excise regulations.

Blending and diluting whiskies are for the
most part done in the bonded warehouses. "All
commercial spirit," says an authority on the subject, "however pure, contains a small proportion
of impurities" (which sounds Irish) "or by-
products of distillation known as fusel-oil." It
will relieve the minds of some to know that fusel-
oil is merely a by-product of distillation, and
not the "low-flash" stuff which causes the
accidents with the cheap lamps. It used to be
thought that during the "maturing," or "age-
ing," of whisky the constituents of fusel-oil
underwent decomposition ; but my good friend
Doctor James Bell, C.B., the chief Government
analyst at Somerset House (he retired some three
years ago), utterly refuted this theory by analysis.

Whisky is, like brandy, naturally white, and

takes its trade colour, and, to a certain extent, flavour, from the sherry-casks in which it is matured. It is also coloured by the direct addition of caramel (burnt sugar), or a maturing wine.

In America, Rye or Bourbon whisky is made from wheat or maize grown in the Bourbon country, Kentucky, and some of it would kill at forty yards. The chief distillery states on the other side of the Atlantic are Illinois, Ohio, Kentucky, Indiana, New York, and Pennsylvania. At the Cape, and throughout South Africa, there is decent whisky procurable, as also a pernicious compound known as "Square-face" or "Cape smoke," and in much favour with the dusky races of the country. On the Congo, palm-wine —similar to the fermented toddy of the East Indies—was for centuries the only livener, but with the march of civilization have come the whiskies of Great Britain, more or less adulterated ; and whereas in the past death by the sword, or the club, was the only known punishment for the subjects of the native tyrants who are so fond of thinning out the population, a well-fuselled whisky is now freely employed for the same purpose.

Although whisky is now freely partaken of all over Great Britain, it was comparatively speaking despised in England until the first half of the present century had slipped by. This fact is apparent from a perusal of contemporary literature. And in no country has "malt" had such a rise in public estimation as in the great continent of Hindustan, where "John Exshaw" and "John

Collins—the last named a seductive compound of gin, limes, Curaçoa, and soda-water—have been almost knocked out by John Barleycorn and Jean Pomme-de-terre. Until the visit of H.R.H. the Prince of Wales, brandy was almost the sole potation of the heroes who helped to hold the big wonderland, the old-fashioned *brandi-pani* gradually giving place to the brandy diluted with *Belati pani*, or "Europe water." Thirty years ago a "peg" meant a brandy-and-soda; but whisky has now usurped the proud position once occupied by the products of John Exshaw, Justerini and Brooks, and others.

CHAPTER VIII

OTHER SPIRITS

Old Jamaica pine-apple—"Tots" for Tommy Atkins—The grog
  tub aboard ship—*Omelette au rhum*—Rum-and-milk—Ditto-
  and-ale — A maddening mixture — Rectifying gin—"The
  seasoning as does it "—Oil of turpentine and table-salt—A
  long thirst—A farthing's worth of Old Tom—Roach-alum
  —Dirty gin—Gin and bitters—"Kosher" rum—An active
  and intelligent officer—Gambling propensities of the Israelites
  —The dice in the tumbler—Nomenclature at "The Olde
  Cheshyre Cheese "—" Rack "—" Cork."

WE now come to Rum, "superior old Jamaica
pine-apple," otherwise known as "sailors' tea"
— the spirit in question having from time
immemorial been held in high esteem by
mariners both afloat and ashore. Rum is
probably one of the easiest beverages to make,
being, simply, fermented and distilled cane-sugar.
Occasionally pine-apples and guavas are thrown
into the still, but in making this spirit on a large
scale no attempts are made to add to its flavour
and thereby deduct from the profits to be made
on the commodity. It is coloured with caramel,
and the longer you keep it the better and, therefore, the more valuable, it becomes. In the city

of Carlisle in 'the year 1865 some rum known to be 140 years old was sold for £3 : 3s. per bottle.

This is not the brand served out to our army and navy; although the "tots" issued periodically to Tommy Atkins and Ben Bowline consist of good, sound liquor, wholesome enough, save for gouty subjects—and a sailor with the gout would be of about as much use to his Queen and country as a watch without works — and writing from past experience I can aver that every drop of liquor, whether ale or rum, supplied in a regimental canteen had to be previously passed by a committee of "taste." In many ships, nowadays, no rum or other intoxicant is served out ; and as no equivalent is given, it might appear as though the owners made a good thing out of the temperate habits of their crews. But I do not believe in total abstinence as an aid to work ; and I have never seen a sailor the worse— on board ship—for his "tot." On the other hand, in the old days of "Green's" troop-ships, the old sailing-vessels which made the voyage to India round the Cape of Good Hope, it was by no means infrequent for a soldier to be "overcome" by the cane-spirit, of which he occasionally got rather more than his orthodox allowance.

How was this managed ? The thrifty sea-farers were in the habit of selling their grog allowance to the "swaddies" ; and as soon as the ship's captain found this out, he issued stringent regulations which it might have been expected would put a stop to this practice. When all hands were piped to grog a ship's officer was stationed by the tub, to see that each sailor drank his allowance. Still there was intoxication amongst the troops, and it was discovered that many of the sailors' pannikins had false bottoms, and that in this way the rum was concealed. After that the ship's officer was enjoined to see that each sailor partook of his tot ; but even this precaution failed ; for the rum would be ejected from the men's mouths into a bucket in the fo'c'sle, and then sold — a disgusting practice which merited severe punishment, and frequently obtained it.

We English do not make nearly as much use of rum in cookery as do our lively neighbours. One of the most approved of *entremets* is an *omelette au rhum*, a truly grateful dish, if the omelette be properly made, although rum be spelt with an "h." But it is a mistake to use rum-sauce with plum-pudding, as do the French ; for brandy is a far better digestive of the cloying materials of which the pudding is composed. As mentioned in *Cakes and Ale*, rum-and-milk is said, by the chief English authority on dietetics, to be the most powerful restorative known to man. This may, or may not, be true ; I am prepared to back a judicious dose of "the Boy"—*not* limited to a "split pint," either. But of all horrible mixtures, defend me from rum-and-ale, which used to be a potion much in favour with the dangerous classes of our metropolis, in the days when I went "slumming" in search of plain unvarnished facts. A steaming tumbler of rum and hot water, with a piece of butter melted therein, was, in my younger days, in vogue as an infallible

specific to eject a cold from the head. Nowadays,
I prefer the cold.

Gin is supposed by students, who do not make
practical test of their learning, to be distilled
from malt, or from unmalted barley, or from
some other grain, and afterwards rectified and
flavoured. And just as it was (according to
Mr. Samuel Weller) the seasoning which did it
in the case of the cheap pies, so is it the rectifying, and the flavouring which do it, in the matter
of gin. Occasionally "rectifying" is hardly the
right word to use. That there is such a thing
as wholesome, tolerably-pure gin is more than
probable ; but there is also a very undesirable
fluid sold to the poorer classes, and esteemed by
their vitiated palates, known under different pet
names, of which "blue ruin" and "white satin"
are two. This brand of gin is flavoured more or
less with oil of turpentine and common salt.
No wonder thirst stalks abroad next morning !

"In one well-known hostelry," observes a
writer in a daily newspaper, "situated not a stone's
throw from the Bank of England, you can, if
you be so minded, ask for and obtain a farthing's
worth of gin. It is served in tiny liqueur-glasses,
and the custom dates from the time when the
purchasing power of the coin in question was
far greater than it is now, and when, consequently, a farthing's worth of gin was considered
to be a sufficient quantity for any respectable
citizen. Another public-house, in Bishopsgate
Street, is also compelled, by the terms of its
license, to supply a farthing's worth of either
'gin, rum, or shrub,' to any customer requiring

it ; while not far away is a hostelry which is
permitted to carry on the dual businesses of
liquor-dispensing or pawnbroking. Yet another
City public-house possesses a sort of annexe
where medicines are retailed. Handy, this, for
the unhappy sufferer from swelled head."

I suppose as the above has appeared in a newspaper, it is strictly true. But how sad ! Although my knowledge of London is " peculiar "
I cannot say I am acquainted with the licensed
house in which drawing drinks and taking in
pledges are combined ; but I have seen farthing's
worths of " Old Tom " dispensed in more than
one hostelry, to slatternly women, before my
own breakfast hour, and I have shuddered at the
sight. But why stop short at selling medicines
in the annexe of a dram shop ? I should have
thought an undertaker, in another compartment,
might do a fairish trade.

These are some of the ingredients put into
gin, to give it " body," and make it " bite "—gin
without teeth being notoriously inferior tipple
and altogether unfit for the consumption of the
good ladies who are, sad to say, by far the best
customers of the gin retailer :—roach-alum (this
sounds fishy), salt of tartar, oil of juniper, cassia,
nutmeg, lemon, fennel, and carraway and coriander seeds, cardamoms, capsicums, and sulphuric
acid. All these, mind ye, besides the aforementioned oil of turpentine, and the aforementioned potato-spirit, which last would seem
to enter into most drinks of the day.

The word " Gin " is really an abbreviation of
" Geneva," under which name the spirit was at

one time known. Not that it is principally
manufactured in picturesque Switzerland, where
the watches come from ; but " Geneva " is a
corruption of the old French word *genevre*, the
juniper. I used to read, in childhood's days, that

Juniper berries and barley make gin,

but those ingredients—or the berries, at all
events—would seem to be only regularly used in
Holland, nowadays.

" Dirty " gin, of which we used to hear so
much, was, I believe, as pure as any other
geneva, and not less clean. Plymouth gin is
said to be the healthiest form of the article, but
'tis an acquired taste, and " Old Tom " is certainly more toothsome. In entering as fully
into details as I have above I have no wish to
discourage the consumption of gin proper, especially when blended with ginger-beer (an excellent
summer beverage), or doing duty in a cock-tail,
a sling, a punch, or a John Collins. But I am
not a " gin man " myself. And to my mind a
" nip " less calculated to promote appetite than
any other is a " gin-and-bitters."

" Kosher " rum, *i.e.* rum treated according to
instructions laid down in the Mosaic Law, is in
high favour with the Jews ; and in some of the
taverns which abut on the Israelitish quarters
which are about Aldgate there are recognized
" rum-rooms." There used to be, and probably
is at the present day, a considerable amount of
card-playing (*spieling*) or throwing of dice for
wagers, carried on in these apartments ; and I
once knew a son of Judah who was heavily fined

by the stipendiary magistrate, for gambling on licensed premises. To the day of his death this Jew protested his innocence of the crime.

He told me the whole story, interlarded with tears and gesticulations.

The *rozzers* (detectives) raided the rum-room one afternoon, and created considerable commotion. Some of the imbibers managed to make their escape, but my informant was not so fortunate. He was seized by one minion of the law, and shortly afterwards another officer cried:

"See where he has hidden the dice in his tumbler of Old Jamaica!"

"And, may I die," added the poor Yid, "if the *gonoph* (rascal) hadn't placed 'em there himself—don't yer beliefe me?"

Of course I did.

Here is another way of employing rum; but you will not be able to shine at solo-whist afterwards.

Rum Booze.

The yolks of eight eggs well beaten up, with some sifted sugar, and a grated nutmeg; extract the juice from rind of a lemon by rubbing loaf sugar thereon; put the sugar, a piece of cinnamon, and a bottle of white wine into a clean saucepan, and when the wine boils take it off the fire. Pour one glass of cold sherry into it, put it into a spouted jug (I don't mean hypothecated, but a jug with a spout to it) and pour it gradually amongst the egg mixture, keeping the whole well stirred with a spoon as the wine is poured in. Sweeten to taste, and pour the mixture from one vessel to another until a fine white froth is obtained.

The recipe continues : " Half a pint of rum is sometimes added, but it is then very intoxicating."

But *sans* rum whence the Rum Booze ? Port wine is sometimes substituted for white wine, but is not considered so palatable. This liquor should be drunk when quite hot. If the wine be poured boiling hot among the eggs, the mixture will become curdled.

Without the rum the mixture is one form of Egg Flip.

When treating of gin I should have mentioned that at one well-known City hostelry, " The Olde Cheshyre Cheese " in Wine Office Court, Fleet Street, gin is never known by any other name than " rack." Why, I know not. But in the same old tavern should you require Scotch whisky you must call for " Scotch," without mentioning the word whisky ; and if Irish, " Cork " is the password.

CHAPTER IX

CUPS WHICH CHEER

Claret combinations—Not too much noyeau—A treat for schoolboys—The properties of borage—"Away with melancholy"
—*Salmon's Household Companion*—Balm for vapours—
Crimean cup—An elaborate and far-reaching compound—
Orgeat—A race-day cup—"Should auld acquaintance be
forgot?"—Sparkling Isabella—Rochester's delight—Free-
mason's relish—Porter cup—Dainty drink for a tennis-
party.

IT is probable that there are almost as many
recipes for claret cup as there are letters in Holy
Writ, or acres in Yorkshire. This is the
late Mr.

Donald's Cup.

One bottle claret.
1 wine-glass pale brandy.
$\frac{1}{2}$ do.   yellow chartreuse.
$\frac{1}{2}$ do.   curaçoa.
$\frac{1}{2}$ do.   maraschino.
2 bottles Seltzer water.
1 lemon cut in thin slices.
A few sprigs of borage.
Ice and sugar to taste.

To my taste there is rather too much liqueur in the above. Here is a simple recipe for

Badminton.

Peel half a small cucumber and put it into a silver cup together with four ounces of sifted sugar, the juice of one lemon, a little nutmeg, half a glass of curaçoa, and a bottle of claret ; when the sugar is thoroughly dissolved, pour in a bottle of soda-water, add ice, and drink. The cucumber should not be left in too long, and a sprig or two of borage will improve the flavour.

Balaclava Cup.

Throw into a large bowl the thinly pared rind of half a lemon, add two tablespoonfuls of sifted sugar, the juice of two lemons, and half a small cucumber, *unpeeled*, in slices. Mix well, and add two bottles of soda-water, two bottles of claret, and one of champagne ; mix well, ice, and flavour with borage.

Another Claret Cup.

Put into a large bowl three bottles of claret, a large wine-glass of curaçoa, a pint of dry sherry, half a pint of old brandy, a large wine-glass of raspberry syrup, three oranges and one lemon cut into slices. Add four bottles of aërated water, sweeten to taste, ice and flavour with borage. This is a good cup for a garden-party, or a tent at Ascot ; and re-member always that the better the ingredients the better the cup. More especially let your brandy be of the right brand.

Yet Another.

Pour into a large jug one bottle of claret, two wine-glasses of dry sherry, and a dash of maraschino.

Add a few sliced nectarines, or peaches, and sweeten to taste. Let it stand till the sugar is melted, and then add a sprig of borage. Just before using add one bottle of Seltzer water, and a large piece of ice.

Soda-water, Stretton water, or any other natural spring-water may be substituted for Seltzer.

One More,

and a very simple one. Put into a bowl the rind of one lemon pared very thin, add sugar to taste, and pour over it a wine-glass of sherry; then add a bottle of claret, more sugar, a sprig of verbena for flavour, one bottle of aërated water, and a little grated nutmeg; strain and ice.

My Ideal Claret Cup.

Two wine-glasses old brandy, one wine-glass curaçoa, and a little thin lemon-peel, sweeten to taste, and pour over the mixture two bottles of light claret. Just before using add a pint bottle of sparkling moselle, and two bottles of fizzing water. Flavour with borage, and put a large block of ice in the bowl.

Nobody who has not tried it can understand how much the addition of a little sparkling Moselle improves a claret cup.

" For'ard On " Cup.

Put into a large bowl three bottles of claret, a *large* wine-glass of curaçoa, one pint of sherry, half a pint of old brandy, two wine-glasses of raspberry syrup, three oranges and one lemon cut into slices; add a few sprigs of borage, a little cucumber-rind, two bottles of Seltzer water and three bottles of soda-water. Mix well, and sweeten to taste. Let the mixture stand for an hour, then strain, and put a large block of ice in it. Serve in small tumblers ; and if champagne be substituted for claret, and noyeau for raspberry syrup, a most excellent champagne cup will be the result. Beware, however, of too free a hand with the noyeau. This liqueur contains hydrocyanic (otherwise Prussic) acid, and should only be used cautiously, unless evil be wished to your guests.

Cider Cup, or Cold Tankard.

This is a favourite beverage for schoolboys and university students. I cannot say that I have encountered it since the early sixties, but 'tis a refreshing drink for the river-side and the cricket-field.

Extract the juice from the peel of one lemon by rubbing loaf-sugar on it ; cut two lemons into thin slices ; the rind of one lemon cut thin, a quarter of a pound of loaf-sugar, and half a pint of brandy (I don't think they allowed as much brandy as this at my old school). Pour the whole into a large jug, mix it well together, and pour one quart of cold spring-water upon it. Grate a nutmeg into it, add one pint of white wine, and a bottle of cider, sweeten to taste with capillaire or sugar, put a handful of balm and the same quantity of borage in flower, stalk downwards. Then put the jug containing this liquor into a tub of ice, and when it has remained there one hour it will be fit for use. The balm and borage should be fresh gathered. And here a few words as to the virtues of these.

In *Evelyn's Acetaria* it is written :—" The

sprigs of borage in wine are of known virtue, to revive the hypochondriac, and cheer the hard student."

Salmon's Household Companion, 1710, told us : " Borage is one of the four cordial flowers ; it comforts the heart, cheers melancholy, and revives the fainting spirits."

" Borage," wrote Sir John Hill, M.D., " has the credit of being a great cordial ; throwing it into cold wine is better than all the medicinal preparations."

" The leaves, flowers, and seeds of borage," says the *English Physician*, " all or any of them, are good to expel pensiveness and melancholy."

" Balm is very good to help digestion and open obstructions of the brain, and hath so much purging quality in it, as to expel those melancholy vapours from the spirits and blood which are in the heart and arteries, although it cannot do so in other parts of the body " (*Ibid*).

After all this information, let not the garden of the melancholy vapourer be searched in vain for balm and borage.

Perry Cup

is made in the same manner as the above, with the natural substitution of perry for cider.

Crimean Cup.

This is an elaborate affair.

One quart of syrup of orgeat (to make this *vide* next recipe), one pint and a half of old brandy, two wine-glasses of maraschino, one pint of old rum, two large and one small bottles of champagne, three bottles of Seltzer water, half a pound of sifted sugar, and the juice of five lemons. Peel the lemons and put the thin rind in a mortar with the sugar. Pound them well, and scrape the result with a silver spoon into a large bowl. Squeeze in the juice of the lemons, add the Seltzer water, and stir till the sugar is quite dissolved. Then add the orgeat, and whip the mixture well with a whisk, so as to whiten it. Add the maraschino, rum, and brandy, and strain the whole into another bowl. Just before the cup is required, put in the champagne and stir vigorously with a punch ladle. The champagne should have been previously well iced, as no apparent iceberg is allowable in this mixture.

Do not make too free with this mixture, if you are about to ride the favourite for an important race, or you will be seeing five winning posts, like the late " Jem " Snowden.

Orgeat.

You do not often hear this compound called for nowadays, but here is the programme for its manufacture :—

Blanch and pound three quarters of a pound of sweet almonds, and thirty bitter almonds, in one tablespoonful of water. Stir in by degrees two pints of water and three pints of milk. Strain the mixture through a cloth. Dissolve · half a pound of loaf-sugar in one pint of water. Boil and skim well, and then mix with the almond water. Add two tablespoonfuls of orange-flower water and half a pint of old brandy. Be careful to boil the *eau sucré* well, as this concoction must not be too watery.

A Crimean Cup for a much smaller party can be made, without the addition of orgeat, as follows :—

Put the peel of half a lemon or orange into a bowl, add a tablespoonful of sifted sugar, one small glassful of maraschino, half that quantity of curaçoa, and a wine-glassful of old brandy. Mix well together, and add two bottles of aërated water, one bottle of champagne, and a block of ice.

Race-day Cup.

Dissolve a quarter of a pound of sugar in a quarter of a pint of water, add the juice of two lemons, one wine-glassful of brandy, half a wine-glassful of cherry brandy, a dash of maraschino, and a bottle of champagne. Add also a small piece of cucumber-peel, two sprigs of borage, two thin slices of lemon, four strawberries, four brandy-cherries, and two bottles of Seltzer water ; stir well, and ice for an hour after covering up the bowl. Before serving put in a block of ice, and serve in tumblers.

Loving Cup.

Better a little flavoured brandy-and-water where love is than a Crimean Cup or a Halo Punch amidst bickerings and vexation of spirit.

Rub the rind of two oranges on loaf-sugar and put the sugar into a bowl ; add half a pint of brandy, the juice of one lemon, one-third of a pint of orange juice, and one pint of water. Add more sugar if required, and ice well.

I don't know if the above is the way the Loving Cup at the Mansion House is made ;

H

but probably one recipe is as good as another, when all you have to do is to sip the liquid and pass it on.

The ancients knew not " cups "; simply because they knew not the virtues of Wenham Lake ice, or its imitations ; whilst the "strong-waters " and alleged wines of the past did not blend particularly well, and there was no soda-water. Fearful and wonderful beverages were their compound drinks, however, many of which have already been analysed in these pages. But the recipe for

Rochester

Cup, which is taken from a comparatively modern book, smacks of the antique. At all events my own wine-merchant professes to be "out of" sparkling Catawba and sparkling Isabella. But here is the programme.

Put into a bowl two bottles of sparkling Catawba, two bottles of sparkling Isabella, and one bottle of Sauterne ; mix well, then add two wine-glasses of maraschino and two wine-glasses of curaçoa ; ice well, and add some strawberries, or a few drops of extract of peach or vanilla.

A very excellent

Champagne Cup

can be made from the recipe headed " Donald's Cup " at the commencement of this chapter, substituting "the Boy" for the red wine of Bordeaux. And here is a simple little refresher, suitable for a breaking-up party at a young ladies' school,

Chablis Cup.

Dissolve four or five lumps of sugar in a quarter
of a pint of boiling water, and put it into a bowl
with a very thin slice of lemon rind ; let it stand
for half an hour, then add a bottle of chablis, a sprig
of verbena, a wine-glassful of sherry, and half a pint
of water. Mix well, and let the mixture stand for
a while, then strain, add a bottle of Seltzer water, a
few strawberries or raspberries, and a block of ice.
Serve in small glasses.

Should you wish to make

Red Cup

use one pint of port wine instead of white ; and
sometimes two glasses of red-currant jelly are added.
In other respects, follow the directions already laid
down for making Cider Cup ; a little warm water
being necessary to dissolve the jelly.

Freemason.

This sounds a "for'ard" sort of potion :—Put
into a bowl one pint of Scotch ale, one pint of mild
ale, half a pint of brandy, one pint of sherry, and
half a pound of sifted sugar. Mix well together,
grate a little nutmeg over the top, and add a block
of ice.

Mind, I, personally, do not believe in the
blending of malt liquor with wine or spirits ;
and the above reads like a bile-provoker of the
most persistent type. But compared with the
next recipe—which some of my readers may
think should come, for choice, under the heading
of "Strange Swallows"—it is harmless indeed.

Porter Cup.

Put into a tankard or covered jug one bottle of
stout, one bottle of mild ale, and one wine-glassful
of old brandy, with sugar *ad lib.;* then add a little
powdered ginger, half a nutmeg grated ; cover it
over, ice for half an hour ; before serving, stir in a
teaspoonful of carbonate of soda, add a few strips of
cucumber-rind, and put in, last of all, a block of ice.

One more cup, and I have done with this
part of my subject.   This is a ladylike concoction,
as its name would seem to imply.

Tennis Cup.

Put into a bowl four tablespoonfuls of sifted
sugar, the rind of one lemon and juice of two, one
wine-glassful of brandy, one wine-glassful of ginger
syrup, and a small piece of cucumber-rind ; add two
bottles of soda-water, one sprig of borage, and two
sprigs of verbena.   Ice well ; and serve in small
glasses.

CHAPTER X

PUNCH

Derivation of the word questioned—Not an Asiatic drink—" Pale-punts "—No relation to pale punters—Properties of rum—Toddy as a tonic—Irish punch—Glasgie ditto—O'er muckle cauld watter—One to seven—Hech sirs !—Classical sherbet —Virtues of the feet of calves—West India dry gripes—Make your own punch—No deputy allowed—Attraction of capillaire — Gin punch — Eight recipes for milk punch—University heart-cheerers.

> When e'en a bowl of punch we make,
>   Four striking opposites we take :
> The strong, the small, the sharp, the sweet,
>   Together mix'd, most kindly meet,
> And when they happily unite
>   The bowl is pregnant with delight.

IN *Cakes and Ale*, grave doubts are expressed as to whether the usually-accepted derivation of punch is the correct one. Why Asia should be raked to find a name for a purely European con-coction, is beyond my powers of argument ; and, as observed in another place, in the concoction of this seductive brew it is by no means necessary to limit oneself to *five* ingredients.

It may be news to the adopters of the *panch* (five) theory to read that punch was at one time

called "pale-punts," why or wherefore deponent
sayeth not ; here is the extract from a work published A.D. 1691 :—

"Pale-punts, here vulgarly known by the
name of Punch ; a drink compounded of brandy
or *aqua vitæ*, juice of lemons, oranges, sugar, or
such like ; very usual amongst those that frequent
the sea, where a bowl of punch is an usual
beverage."

But it was " usual " only in the days of sailing-
ships and long voyages ; and with fast steamers
and whole evenings devoted to the beauties of
poker, or selling pools, a more usual modern
maritime drink is a modicum of whisky diluted
with aërated water.

"The liquor called Punch," writes another
professional authority, "has become so truly
English, it is often supposed to be indigenous to
this country, though its name at least is Oriental.
The Persian *punj*, or Sanscrit *pancha*, i.e. five
(vide *Fryer's Travels*), is the etymon of its title,
and denotes the number of ingredients of which
it is composed. Addison's 'fox-hunter,' who
testified so much surprise when he found that of
the materials of which this 'truly English'
beverage was made only the water belonged to
England, would have been still more astonished
had his informant also told him that it derived
even its name from the East."

But did natives of the East drink it ? Tell
me that.

"Various opinions are entertained respecting
this compound drink. Some authors praise it as
a cooling and refreshing beverage, when drunk

in moderation ; others condemn the use of it as prejudicial to the brain and nervous system. Dr. Cheyne, a celebrated Scotch physician, author of an essay on 'Long Life and Health,' and who by a system of diet and regimen reduced himself from the enormous weight of thirty-two stone to nearly one-third, which enabled him to live to the age of seventy-two, insists that there is but one wholesome ingredient in it, and that is the water. Dr. Willich, on the contrary, asserts that if a proper quantity of acid be used in making punch, it is an excellent antiseptic, and well calculated to supply the place of wine in resisting putrefaction, especially if drank cold with plenty of sugar ; it also promotes perspiration ; but if drank hot and immoderately it creates acidity in the stomach, weakens the nerves, and gives rise to complaints of the breast. He further states that after a heavy meal it is improper, as it may check digestion, and injure the stomach.

" Rennie states that he once heard a facetious physician at a public hospital prescribe for a poor fellow sinking under the atrophy of starvation a bowl of punch. Mr. Wadd gives us a prescription :—

" ' Rum, aqua dulci miscetur acetum, et fiet ex tali fœdere nobile Punch.'

" He also states that toddy, or punch without acid, when made for a day or two before it is used, is a good and cheap substitute for wine as a tonic, in convalescence from typhus fever, etc."

It is here worthy of note that what is meant by "punch" in Ireland is, and has been for at least two centuries, whisky, sugar, lemon, and

the less water the better. A very old way of
concocting it is to melt the sugar within the
tumbler (which should be covered, *pro tem.*) with
the smallest quantity of water sufficient for the
purpose, the thin lemon-rind having been
previously added. Then comes the whisky;
"and," according to the old formula, "the laste
dhrop o' wather" added atop of the "crathur"
will spoil the punch. But in all English works
in which punch has been mentioned—previous
to the early seventies, at all events—by the active
ingredients of punch should be understood either
rum, brandy, or gin.

"*English Punch*,"

says a writer of our own time, "is, as regards the
spirit, mostly of two kinds — brandy and rum,
mixed in proportions which must be left to taste.
The rum generally predominates. The acid is
nearly always lemon juice. The spice is nearly
always lemon - peel, but sometimes tea - leaf"—
now marry come up!—"sometimes nutmeg; and
as for the sugar and the water they explain themselves."

The Scotch make toddy in very much the
same way as the Irish concoct their punch. But

Glasgow Punch,

according to John Gibson Lockhart, was compounded with the coldest spring-water—a commodity which would seem to be growing somewhat scarce in Caledonia — for the purpose of
punch-making, at all events.

The sugar being melted with a little cold water, the artist squeezed about a dozen lemons through a wooden strainer, and then poured in water enough almost to fill the bowl. In this state the liquor goes by the name of sherbet, and a few of the connoisseurs in his immediate neighbourhood were requested to give their opinion of it—for in the mixing of the sherbet lies, according to the Glasgow creed at least, one half of the whole battle. This being approved by an audible smack from the lips of the umpires, the rum was added to the beverage, I suppose in something about the proportion of one to seven———.

Hech sirs! Or does it mean seven of rum to one of the spring?

Last of all the maker cut a few limes, and running each section rapidly round the rim of his bowl, squeezed in enough of this more delicate acid to flavour the whole composition. In this consists the true *tour-de-maître* of the punch-maker.

Oxford Punch

or

Classical Sherbet

is a very ancient beverage, and from the sustaining powers of the calves'-foot jelly (under what heading, amongst punch ingredients, does this come, by the way?) inserted therein might fairly pose as meat and drink.

Extract the juice from the rind of three lemons, by rubbing loaf-sugar on them. The peeling of two Seville oranges and two lemons, cut extremely thin. The juice of four Seville oranges and ten lemons. Six glasses of calves'-feet jelly in a liquid state. The above to be put into a jug and stirred well together. Pour two quarts of boiling water on the mixture, cover the jug closely, and place it near the fire for a quarter of an hour. Then strain the liquid through a sieve into a punch bowl or jug, sweeten it with a bottle of capillaire (the recipe for this follows), and add half a pint of white wine, a pint of French brandy, a pint of Jamaica rum, and a bottle of orange shrub ; the mixture to be stirred as the spirits are poured in. If not sufficiently sweet, add loaf-sugar, or a little more capillaire. To be served either hot or cold.

In making the punch limes are sometimes used instead of lemons, but are not so wholesome ; in fact Arbuthnot, in his work on aliments, says : " The West India dry gripes are occasioned by lime - juice in punch." And nobody wants them.

Ignorant servants sometimes put oxalic acid into punch, to give it a flavour ; but unless the throats of the drinkers be lined with brass, this acid is of no real service. And the host who would entrust the making of any sort of punch to a subordinate, must be either very ignorant, or very careless of the comfort of his guests—and possibly both. Cups, punches, and salads should always be concocted by somebody who will make personal trial of their merits.

To make

Capillaire,

put two ounces of freshly-gathered maidenhair fern into a jug, with sufficient boiling water to cover it.

Let it stand in front of the fire to infuse for some hours ; then strain and put it into a clear syrup made by boiling together three pounds of sugar and three pints of water ; add two tablespoonfuls of orange-flower water, and stir the mixture over the fire for a few minutes. Strain through a jelly-bag, and bottle when cold.

A more potent punch can be made from the same recipe as the Oxford Punch, by leaving out the calves'-feet jelly, and substituting green tea for water. And this sort is invariably drunk hot. Mix three wine-glasses of noyeau with the original recipe and it is entitled to the name of

Noyeau Punch.

Omit the rum, brandy, and shrub, and substitute two bottles of gin, and it becomes

Gin Punch.

If I could only afford to keep a secretary, a clever stenographer and type-writer, I might be able to supply the world with gratuitous recipes for cooling cups, dainty drinks, and peerless punches, and earn, maybe, the thanks of both Houses of Parliament, and a granite bust on the Thames Embankment or in Shaftesbury Avenue. It is entirely due to lack of funds that I am issuing books on the subject of meat and drink ; and I will now proceed to enlighten the thousands of alleged *bons-vivants*, who ask questions as to the concoction of

Milk Punch.

There are many recipes for this seductive drink, each one better than its predecessor.

1. Warm two quarts of water and one of new milk, then mix them well together, and sweeten with a sufficient quantity of loaf-sugar. Rub a few lumps of sugar on the peel of a lemon, put them into a jug with the above, and half a pint of lemon juice, stirring the mixture well as it is poured in. Then add one quart of old brandy. Strain and bottle off, and in cold weather it will keep a fortnight.

2. Dissolve two pounds and a half of sugar in one gallon of cold spring-water ; add thereto a quarter of a pint of orange-flower water, with the juice of twenty limes and eight oranges. Stir well together ; pour one quart of boiling milk into it, and then add three bottles of old brandy, and a like quantity of orange brandy shrub. Strain and bottle off.

3. Cut the peeling of six Seville oranges and six lemons very thin. Pound in a stone mortar. Add one pint of brandy and let the mixture stand six hours, covered. Then squeeze in the juice of six Seville oranges and eight lemons. Stir well, and add three more pints of brandy, three pints of rum, and three quarts of water. Make two quarts of milk boiling hot, and grate a nutmeg into it ; mix this gradually with the other ingredients, and add a sufficient quantity of loaf-sugar to sweeten it—about two pounds. Stir till the sugar is dissolved ; let the mixture stand twelve hours, then strain through a jelly-bag until quite clear. Bottle off, and it will keep in any climate for any length of time.

4.   Three bottles of rum.
           One bottle of sherry.
           Three pounds of loaf-sugar.
The rind of six lemons and the juice of twelve.
           One quart of boiling skim milk.
Mix together, and let the mixture stand eight days,

stirring it each day. Strain and bottle, and let it stand three months. Then re-bottle, and let the bottles lie on their sides in the cellar for two years, to mature. The flavour will be much better than if drunk after the first period of three months.

5. For a solitary drink.

Put into a small tumbler a teaspoonful of sugar, half a wine-glassful of old brandy, half a wine-glassful of old rum, and fill up with boiling milk.

6. Put into a bottle of rum or brandy the thinly-pared rinds of three Seville oranges, and three lemons. Cork tightly for two days. Rub off on two pounds loaf-sugar the rinds of six lemons, squeeze the juice of the fruit over the two pounds sugar, add one quart of boiling water, and one of boiling milk. Mix well till the sugar is dissolved, and grate a little nutmeg over the mixture. Pour in the rum or brandy, stir, and strain till clear : bottle off.

7. Cut off the thin yellow rind of four lemons and one Seville orange, taking care not to include even a fragment of the *white* rind, and place in a basin. Pour in a bottle of old rum, and let it stand, covered over, for twelve hours. Then strain, and mix with it one pint of lemon juice, and two pints of cold water, in which one pound of sugar-candy has been dissolved ; add the whites of two eggs, beaten to a froth, three pints more of rum, one pint of madeira, one pint of strong green tea, and a wine-glassful of maraschino. Mix thoroughly, and pour over all one pint of boiling milk. Let the punch stand a little while, then strain through a jelly-bag, and either use at once (as you will naturally feel inclined) or bottle off for festivals.

It is assumed, by the compiler of this little volume, that the *best* materials only will be used by the concocters of these compound drinks.

8, and last. The best recipe for milk punch extant. Over the yellow rinds of four lemons and one Seville orange pour one pint of rum. Let it stand, covered over, for twelve hours. Strain and mix in two pints more of rum, one pint of brandy, one pint of sherry, half a pint of lemon juice, the expressed juice of a peeled pine-apple, one pint of green tea, one pound of sugar dissolved in one quart of boiling water, the whites of two eggs beaten up, one quart of boiling milk. Mix well, let it cool, strain through a jelly-bag, and drink, or bottle off.

Restorative Punch.

[This is another Oxford recipe, and used to be the favourite potion of the embryo Gladstones and Roseberies, before proceeding to discuss the affairs of the nation at the " Union." There is " no offence in't."]

Extract the juice from the peeling of one Seville orange and one lemon ; the juice of six Seville oranges and six lemons, six glasses of calves'-feet jelly in a liquid state, and about half a pound of loaf-sugar ; put the whole into a jug, pour on it one quart of boiling water, and then add one pint of old brandy. Stir well together, and use.

Almond Punch.

Extract the juice from the peeling of one Seville orange and one lemon by rubbing loaf-sugar on them ; the juice of six lemons and one Seville orange, one bottle of capillaire, and a quarter of a pound of loaf-sugar. Put the whole into a jug, and when well mixed pour upon it three pints of boiling

water. Cover the jug close, and keep it near the
fire for a quarter of an hour. Then add three ounces
of sweet, and half an ounce of bitter, almonds,
blanched and pounded fine in a mortar, and gradually mixed with a bottle of old brandy. Stir well,
and it may be used immediately.

Egg Punch.

[Also once a favourite beverage at the
universities.]

One quart of cold water, the juice of six lemons
and six oranges, four glasses of calves'-feet jelly in a
liquid state ; stir the whole well together ; let it
remain covered over for half an hour, then strain
through a hair sieve, and add one bottle of capillaire,
two glasses of sherry, half a pint of brandy, and one
bottle of orange shrub. Put some pulverized sugar
and ten fresh hens' eggs into a bowl, beat them well
together, and gradually unite the two mixtures by
keeping the eggs well stirred as it is poured in ; then
whip it with a whisk until a fine froth rises, and if
sweet enough it is fit for immediate use.

This punch should be drunk as soon as made, for
it will not keep sweet.

Omit the wine and spirits, and freeze the re-
mainder, and a delicious mould of ice may be
obtained.

The above can be converted into

Shrub Punch,

of a superior quality, by the simple omission of
the eggs.

Details are wanting as to the composition of
the

Rack Punch

of which Jos. Sedley partook so freely at Vauxhall, and which put a temporary stop to the
carryings-on of the fascinating Miss Sharp with
the susceptible Anglo-Indian. Thackeray does
not tell us if this was an abbreviation of
Arrack Punch. My own idea is that brandy
and rum—of inferior quality—entered into it;
although, as mentioned in a previous chapter,
" rack" is the " Cheshyre Cheese" synonym for
gin. But I should be inclined to back arrack.
At all events this is one of the component
parts of a

Vauxhall Punch

of which the recipe is in my possession.

A large tumbler, one wine-glass of old brandy,
one ditto of old rum, one ditto of arrack, the juice
of half a lemon, and a tablespoonful of sugar.
Mix, strain into two small tumblers, and fill up each
with boiling water.

Uncle Toby.

Here is another encouragement to the bile
industry :—

Rub the rind of one lemon on two lumps of
sugar, put the sugar in a large tumbler with the
juice of the lemon, and dissolve in one wine-glass of
boiling water; then add one wine-glass of brandy,
one ditto of rum, and two dittoes of hot stout; mix
well, strain, and add more sugar if necessary.

Victoria Punch.

Throw into a bowl one lemon cut in slices, free
from pips, two ounces of sifted sugar, two wine-
glasses of boiling water, one wine-glass of hot milk,
one wine-glass of old rum, and one ditto of ancient
brandy ; keep stirring whilst adding the ingredients ;
strain and serve.

Yorkshire Punch.

I have not yet met this in the North Riding;
but it is never too late to copy a good recipe.

Rub the rinds of three lemons on a quarter of a
pound of lump-sugar, and place the sugar in a bowl
with the thin rind of one lemon and of one orange,
the juice of four oranges and of ten lemons, six wine-
glasses of calves'-feet jelly, and two quarts of boiling
water. Mix thoroughly, strain, and add a pint of
rum, a pint of brandy, and a bottle of orange shrub.
Sweeten to taste.

Champagne Punch.

Pare two lemons very thin, and steep the peel in
one pint of rum.   Add a wine-glass of sherry, half a
pint of brandy, the juice of four lemons, a little
capillaire, as much boiling water as you may fancy
—play light with the kettle, lads—sweeten to taste,
and last thing of all pour in a bottle of champagne.

The above will act as a restorative after a
hard day's hunting. Later in the evening the
true sportsman may feel ready and willing to
tackle a glass or two of the celebrated

I

Halo Punch,

whose praises continue to be sung throughout the land.

With a quarter of a pound of sugar rub off the outer rind of one lemon and two Seville oranges. Put rind and sugar into a large punch bowl with the juice and pulp ; mix the sugar well with the juice and one teacupful of boiling water (just enough to melt it) and stir till cold.

Add half a pint of pine-apple syrup, one pint of strong green tea, a wine-glass of maraschino, a liqueur-glass of noyeau, half a pint of " Liquid Sunshine " rum, one pint of old brandy, and a bottle and a half of " the Boy." Sweeten to taste, strain, and serve.

Do not, oh ! do not boil the above before serving, as did some Cleveland friends of mine, on the night of a certain Ebor Handicap. The result of this was a considerable amount of chaos.

The above was the favourite tipple of the Prince Regent at the beginning of the present century.

CHAPTER XI

STRANGE SWALLOWS

" Wormwood ! "—The little green fairy—All right when you
know it, but—— —The hour of absinthe—Awful effects—
Marie Corelli—St. John the Divine—Arrack and bhang not
to be encouraged—Plain water—The original intoxicant—
Sacred beverage of the mild Hindu—Chi Chi—Kafta, an
Arabian delight—Friends as whisky agents—Effervescent
Glenlivet—The peat-reek—American bar-keeper and his
best customer—" Like swallerin' a circ'lar saw and pullin' it
up again "—Castor-oil anecdote—" Haste to the wedding ! "

WE will now proceed to consider certain weird
potations, some of which I have personally tested,
others of which not all the wealth of Golconda,
Peru, and Throgmorton Street would induce me
to sample of my own accord, and all of which
bring more or less trouble in their wake.

Gall and wormwood have been closely allied
from time immemorial ; and it is in accordance
with the eternal fitness of things that the consumption of

Absinthe

should be almost entirely confined to France.
And what is absinthe ? Merely alcohol, in

which have been macerated for a week or so the pounded leaves and flowering tops of wormwood, together with angelica root, sweet-flag root, star-anise, and other aromatics. The liquor is then distilled, and the result is the decoctions sacred to the " little green fairy," who has accomplished even more manslaughter than the Mahdi, the Khalifa, and the Peculiar People, put together. Of all the liqueurs absinthe is the most pernicious ; and with many other sins it occupies some time in taking possession of its victim. Like Mr. Chevalier's hero, you " have to know it fust," and after that the rest is easy. Like golf, " scorching," and gambling, once you " get " absinthe, it gets you, and never leaves you whilst you last ; and there is a weird, almost tragic, look about the milky liquid, when diluted with water, as to suggest smoke, and brimstone, and flames, with a demon rising from their midst. But it is only " the little green fairy " ; who is, however, as deadly and determined as any demon.

The best absinthe is made in the canton of Neuchâtel, Switzerland, and is not made entirely from Wormwood proper, but from a mixture of plants related to it—such as Southernwood (" Old Man "), and another which takes its name from the invulnerable Achilles. But the merry Swiss boy knows a trick worth two of drinking absinthe ; so the French get the most of it, whilst some goes to America, and some to the foreign quarters of our great metropolis. The French soldiers learnt to appreciate it, from drinking it as a febrifuge, during the Algerian campaign, 1832-47, and it afterwards became, gradually, a popular drink on the boulevards, where the five o'clock gossip-hour at the *cafés* came to be known as "the hour of absinthe." Its use is now forbidden in the French army and navy, and no wonder. The evil effects of drinking it are very apparent : utter derangement of the digestive system, weakened frame, limp muscles, pappy brain, jumpy heart, horrible dreams and hallucinations, with paralysis or idiocy to bring down the curtain.

In that seductive, though gruesome book, *Wormwood*, Marie Corelli gives a most graphic picture of an *absintheur*, once a gay young banker, who, through trouble of no ordinary kind, gradually came under the spell of the "green fairy." I forget how many murders he committed ; but his awful experiences and hallucinations will never leave anybody who has read the book. He is haunted for some days by a leopard who accompanies him on his walks abroad, and who lies down at the foot of his bed at night-time—the "jim-jams," in fact, in their worst form.

"There are two terrible verses," says a writer on the subject, "in the Revelations of St. John.

"And the third angel sounded his trumpet, and there fell a great star from the heavens, burning like a lamp, and it fell upon a third part of the rivers and upon the fountains of waters. And the name of the star is called Wormwood ; and the third part of the waters became Wormwood, and many men died of the waters because they were made bitter."

Which seems a very appropriate quotation ;

yet will men drink of the waters, for although
absinthe makes the heart grow blacker, and the
pulse more feeble, men—and, occasionally women
—will continue, as long as there is a world, to do
the thing they ought not to do. With which
moralising let us pass to the next objectionable
drink,

Arrack.

This is an East Indian name, derived from
the Arabic, for all sorts of distilled spirits, but
chiefly for the " toddy," or palm-liquor obtained
from the cocoa-palm, as also from rice, and the
coarse brown sugar known to the natives as
" jaggery." " Toddy," when fresh, is a delicious
drink, and bears no sort of relationship to whisky-
toddy. An almost nude male swarms up a
cocoa-palm—assisted by a rope which encircles
his ankles and the trunk of the tree—early in the
morning, and fetches down the vessel which has
been fastened up atop, overnight, to catch the
sap which has dripped from the incisions made in
the tree. That sap, in its raw state, is delicious
—especially with a dash of rum in it ; but it
ferments rapidly, and usually turns sour in three
or four days. Then the natives distil, and make
" arrack " of it—a liquor which is sold in the
bazaars and drunk on the occasion of a *burra din*,
or festival. Nor is its use confined to natives.
The British soldier drinks it, *faute de mieux ;*
and occasionally the British officer.

Poor B——, who was in my old regiment,
had fuddled himself into such a state of stupidity,
that all liquor was forbidden him by the doctor's

orders. I, who shared his bungalow, took particular care that these orders were carried out, and threatened his *bearer* and *khitmugar* with fearful penalties should they convey any surreptitious alcohol to the *sahib*. Still he managed to get it ; and it took me a week to find out *how*. His *syce* (groom) used to smuggle arrack from the bazaar, and hide it under the horse's bedding in the stable ; and whenever I was away from the house, poor B—— used to creep over to the stable, and "soak" there !

An imitation arrack may be made by dissolving 10 grains of benzoic acid in a pint of rum ; but arrack is just the sort of fluid which ought not to be imitated. Give me the honest, manly, simple, beautiful Bass !

Bhang,

another dreadful East Indian drink, and a deadly intoxicant, is distilled from hemp ; and if it had only been round the neck of the inventor before he invented it, society would have benefited.

Saké,

the favourite beverage of the Japs, who got it from the Chinese, and improved upon it, is not a desirable swallow. It is a rapid intoxicant, but the over-estimator rapidly recovers the perpendicular. *Saké* was handed round as a liqueur, at the much-advertised banquet of the " Thirteen Club " ; but it is said that the liqueur was in no subsequent request. Not even one of those daring and adventurous mirror-smashers and salt-spillers express the desire to take-on *saké* "in a moog."

Vodka

is the "livener" of the Russian peasantry, and is distilled from—what?

Plain Water,

whether fortunately or otherwise, comes under the heading of "Strange Swallows." It is still consumed in prisons, and other places where sinners and paupers are dieted at the expense of the ratepayer. And hard as are the ways of the transgressor, his daily "quencher" is even harder. "Plain water," wrote a celebrated Mongolian of his day, "has a malignant influence, and ought on no account to be drunk." More especially if it be Thames water. I once saw a drop of this, very much magnified, displayed on a stretched cloth, in a side-show at the Crystal Palace. In that drop of water I counted three boa-constrictors, a few horrors which resembled giant lobsters, and a pair of turtles engaged, apparently, in a duel to the death. Three ladies in the front row of the stalls, at that exhibition, were carried out, swooning.

Whether cold water ought to be drunk, or not, I am bound, as a tolerably truthful chronicler, to remark that very few folk who can obtain any other sort of tipple do drink it.

It has been claimed by the Brahmins that

The Orginal Intoxicant

was evolved from the climbing bindweed of Hindustan, one of the convolvulus family. From this was made a liquor called *Soma*, which is still the sacred beverage of the Hindus. It is the Persian *Haoma*, and, I should imagine, "absolutely beastly" to the Christian taste. Everybody knows the Christian bindweed—the stuff you get in your garden when you set potatoes, or early peas.

Pulque, which is the sap of the aloe, is the favourite drink of the Mexicans. In Kamtchatka the natives drink (or used to drink) birch-wine, which has been already described in these pages. The Russians, also, are very fond of birch-wine ; and their's effervesces, like champagne.

In Patagonia they drink

Chi Chi,

a cider made from wild apples. Pits are dug, and lined with the hides of horses, to prevent any liquor escaping, the apples are thrown in, and left to decay, and ferment, "on their own." The Patagonians have an annual "big drink" of this dreadful mess, besides many smaller boosing-bouts. And upon these occasions the Patagonian ladies are in the habit of hiding all the knives and lethal weapons they can find, and retiring, with their children, into the woods, until their lords and masters and other relatives have drunk themselves mad, and then slept themselves sober again.

In the Caucasus district there be strange drinks made from mares' milk, sparkling—such as *Koumiss*, or otherwise. But these beverages do not have a large sale in other districts.

Kafta,

which hardly comes under the heading of " swallows," is in much request amongst the Arabs, especially in the neighbourhood of Yemen. These people boil the leaves and stems of the *kat*—a shrub about ten feet high, which is planted in the same ground as the coffee—and chew them. All visitors are presented with twigs of this *kat* plant to chew ; and the drawing-room carpet suffers terribly.

" Very pleasant sensations " are, it is said, caused by this custom, and the effect is so invigorating that the Arab soldier who goes in steadily for *Kafta* can do " sentry go " all night without feeling in the least drowsy. Whether the soldiers of the Khalifa did much chewing on the night before the battle of Omdurman deponent sayeth not. Frequently the *kat* leaves are boiled in milk sweetened with honey, and the result is the same. The infusion is intoxicating, but the effect is not of long endurance ; and at a synod of the most learned Mahomedans it was pronounced lawful for the faithful to chew, or drink *Kafta,* " as, whilst it did not impair the health nor hinder the observance of religious duties, it increased hilarity and good humour." Sly rogues, these followers of the Prophet !

If a man wants to retain his old friends and

to make fresh ones let not that man take to
selling wines or spirits on commission. Some
years ago I gave an old schoolfellow an order for
a case of Scotch whisky, which he declared upon
oath to be absolutely the best procurable. Home
came the whisky, and the first cork was drawn.
Pop! The stuff was literally effervescent, like
champagne, or Russian birch-wine. "My dear,"
I observed to the partner of my joys and cares,
"we had better not drink much of this."

At the next Sandown Park race-meeting I
met the whisky agent, who, I forgot to mention
before, was a bit of a stammerer.

"And wh-wh-wh-what," he asked, "d'you
think of that wh-wh-wh-wh-whisky?"

Stammering is occasionally to be caught.

"I think," was my reply, "it's the d-d-d-
dashedest m-m-m-muck I ever t-t-t-t-tasted."

"Wh-wh-what's the m-m-m-matter with it?"

"It f-f-f-fizzes like g-g-g-ginger p-p-p-pop."

"My d-d-dear sir," he protested, "that is no
dr-dr-drawback. That's the p-p-p-peat-r-r-reek."

Peat-reek or no, that whisky was not used
for household purposes—not even for the Christmas pudding; but was kept for the special benefit
of such police-constables, Inland Revenue officers,
process-servers, tax-gatherers, book agents, and
retailers of certain winners, as might call around,
with a thirst in them.

Strange whisky reminds me of the American
story of the proprietor of a spirit-store in Arizona,
who found the ordinary brand of "Rye" was not
sufficiently attractive to his customers. So he
fitted together a blend of his own, consisting of

essence of ginger, capsicums, croton oil, snuff, carbolic acid, pain-killer, turpentine, and a little very young and very potent spirit distilled from old junk. He placed a bottle of this on the counter, and the first customer who came along helped himself to a tumblerful, and, taking it "straight," swallowed it at a gulp.

As soon as he had got his second wind, he gasped out : "That's the best doggoned whisky I've sampled in this yer camp. Sonny, guess you've fixed me up to rights. It's like swallerin' a circ'lar saw and pullin' it up again. So long."

And with the tears pouring down his cheeks, and holding on to his diaphragm with both hands, he staggered into the open. The saloon-keeper watched him from the doorway, until he had passed the second block, and rounded the corner ; and returned to his counter and his bottles, with the pious exclamation : "The Lord be praised ! He hasn't died in our parish ! "

No chapter on strange drinks would be complete without the following story, which, I confess at the outset, is one of the most venerable of "chestnuts." It appeared in the *Sporting Times* four-and-twenty years ago, and I will not affirm that it was strictly original even then. It has since been translated into every known language ; but it is just possible that some of the rising generation may not have heard it.

A well-dressed gentleman entered a chemist's shop one morning, evidently in a violent hurry.

"Can you make me up a dose of castor-oil ? "

"Certainly, sir," said the dispenser, with a bow.

Whilst he was going through the usual motions—no prescription can be properly made up until the chemist has overhauled every bottle on the top shelf, opened most of the empty drawers, and upset a tray of tooth-brushes—the customer was fidgeting about the shop, and fanning himself with a scented pocket-handkerchief.

"It's infernally hot," he said presently, "and I don't think I ever felt so thirsty in my life. Can I have a bottle of lemonade?"

"Certainly, sir."

More sorting of bottles. Presently "pop" goes a cork, and the sparkling lemonade is poured into a mammoth tumbler. The customer drains it at once.

"Ah-h-h!" he crowed, wiping his mouth. "I feel a bit better now."

A pause. Presently he asked:—

"Have you made that up yet?"

"What, sir?" asked the chemist.

"Why that stuff—the castor-oil I ordered."

"You've had it, sir."

"Had it! Wotty mean?"

"I gave it you in the lemonade, sir."

"Great Scotland Yard!" exclaimed the customer. "I didn't want it for myself—I'm going to be married in half an hour!"

CHAPTER XII

" SEE how it sparkles, this drink divine,"

sings Giroflé, in Lecocq's opera ; and although
the sparkling liquor therein is described in the
text as " punch "—which does *not* sparkle much
as a rule—I have no doubt whatever that what
Lecocq, or his librettist meant, was the grateful
liquid which is described in different circles of
society as " fiz," "Simpkin" (the nearest approach
a Mahomedan table-servant can make to " champagne ") "a bottle," "golden pop," and "the
Boy."

Here let me interpolate the commonly-received

interpretation of the last-named title. At a shooting party, a stout urchin of some fifteen summers was specially told off to carry the liquid refreshment for the shooters, which took the form of Perrier Jouët in magnums. And so frequent were the calls of "Boy!" that morning, that the youth threw up his situation before noon.

D'you believe it? Not a word of it? Same here. At least I never attended a "shoot" at which the gunners steadied their nerves by the aid of choice vintages—before luncheon, at all events; and I don't mean to begin now. Champagne was probably called "the Boy" because of its free, happy, joyous, loose-and-careless characteristics. The sparkle represents youth, and the froth irresponsibility; whilst the whole—— but never mind about the whole, just now.

The Champagne district, as some people know, lies on the chalk hills which surround the valley of the Marne. The townlets of Epernay, Ay, and Château Thierry owe their prosperity to these seductive wines, and Rheims has attained world-wide celebrity, as much from being the centre of the champagne industry as from being the seat of the premier ecclesiastic of France, the Archbishop of Paris. So far, guide-book.

The champagne-vines are short and stunted, the grapes being small, but most prolific of juice. A third, and even a fourth, crushing will yield a very delicious wine, to an uneducated palate; and this is the inferior liquor which is sold to tourists in Rheims at the equivalent of one shilling and fivepence per large bottle. It is a sweet—what

connoisseurs call a "lady's" wine, which an
expert would not taste a second time ; and its
aftermath, its effect on the imbiber the following
day, is somewhat distressing. Somehow, not-
withstanding the import duties, champagne—I
am alluding now to the superior brands—is
almost as cheap in London as in the best hotels
in Rheims ; but the experiment of drinking it
in the land of its birth is not as risky as on alien
shores. At least so say the natives of the district,
who maintain that although work in the cellars
is not the pleasantest in the world—the strong
smell, which is even intoxicating, giving the
workmen a distaste for the sparkling wine—it is
quite possible for an outsider to drink a quantity
of champagne of undoubted quality without feeling any bad after-effects.

"You may, in fact," it was told me on the
spot, "drink four bottles of Pommery '84, and
feel all the better for it next day."

Possibly ; but how about the inferior stuff
which we used to sample, occasionally, in our
salad days, when our green judgment led us to
pass our early mornings in riotous junketings in
the now staid and peaceful region of the Hay-
market, S.W. ? Much later than those days I
have sampled alleged champagne—"extra sec," it
was called, though "extra sick" would have
been more appropriate—on a race-course, in
order to fitly celebrate some famous victory.
But in my riper years, the victory (when it
occurs) is honoured in more staid and seemly
fashion. I was never nearer death by poison than
one Friday morning in the ancient city of York,

after indulging somewhat freely in the "sparkling" proffered me on the previous day in a
booth on Knavesmire. Do what I would—and
I walked ten miles, went for a scull on the river
Ouse, and then swallowed hot mustard-and-water
—the distressing sensations, the great wave of
depression which seemed to have swamped the
heart, would not quit the body, until—and the
idea came as a bolt from the blue—I had sum-
moned up sufficient strength of mind to enter
the coffee-room of the principal hotel, and
demand a pint of Pommery. It was *not* a hair
of the dog which had bitten me; the mangy
brute from the attention of whose fangs I was
suffering was no sort of relation to the highly-
bred terrier who rooted out the anguish from my
soul. And that small pint was so successful that
another went the same way. And by that time
I had been inspired with nerve enough to face a
charging tiger, unarmed.

Many learned people, including one section
of the medical profession, incline to the belief
that consumption of champagne offers direct encouragement to gout. But there is no such
idea amongst those employed in the cellars of
Moet et Chandon, Geisler, Mum, Pommery, and
other large firms. Not that these workmen are
allowed to drink as much of their own foaming
productions as they have a mind to. As a matter
of fact the wine supplied to the *ouvriers* is the
thin red stuff of the district, resembling inferior
Burgundy, and not of a very elevating nature.
It is not particularly attractive, this life of labour,
for nine or ten hours a day, in a damp, cold

K

cellar some fifty yards below the level of the
street pavements, with occasionally bottles bursting to right and left of you. These cellars are
cut out of the calcareous rock, and were, many of
them, inherited from the Romans; and champagne is such a sensitive, exacting sort of wine
that it must be stored in the very bowels of the
earth, where all is peace and quietude, and where
neither motion nor vibration can reach the
maturing vintages.

At least that is what they tell visitors;
although the only time I have visited champagne
cellars could hardly be called a peaceful experience, owing to the almost continuous bombard-
ment of bursting bottles. And it is said that as
a rule at least 10 per cent of the stored wine is
wasted in this way; whilst in seasons of early
and unusual heat the percentage may rise to as
much as 20, and even 25.

Sparkling champagne—and we are not concerned with the still wine—is the result of a
peculiar treatment during fermentation. During
the winter months the wine is racked-off, and
fined with isinglass; and in the early spring it is
bottled and tightly corked. In order to collect
the sediment in the necks of the bottles these are
placed at first in a sloping condition, with the
corks downward, for a term. In the second
year this sediment requires to be disgorged, or
dégagé-ed. This feat can only be learnt by long
practice, and even then there be workmen who
cannot be safely trusted to shift the sediment,
without shifting a too-large proportion of the
wine itself.

May I confess to the belief that I should never make a good, reliable, valuable disgorger ?

Of course there is art, or knack, in it. The *degager* takes a bottle, cuts the string of the cork, expels the sediment — occasionally without spilling more than a drop or two—and passes the bottle to his neighbour, who fills it up with a liqueur, composed of sugar-candy dissolved in cognac, and flavoured, and with some bright, clarified wine. The bottle is then recorked, by machinery, wired, labelled, and sent about its business.

The fermentation being incomplete at the first bottling of the wine, the carbonic acid gas generated in a confined space—this part comes unadorned, out of a book—exerts pressure on itself, and it thus remains as a liquid in the wine. When this pressure is removed it expands into gas, and thus communicates the sparkling property to champagne. Hence the bombardments.

How do I know all this ? I once paid a visit to the cellars of Pommery et C$^{ie.}$; and my dearest friend asked subsequently what sort of writ of ejectment had to be drawn up to rid them of my presence and thirst. But all joking apart the time was well spent, and the industry is deserving of all the encouragement which it receives. The head cellarman is, literally a host in himself, an old gentleman of aristocratic mien, and portly—or, rather, champagne-ly—presence ; and one of the *formulae* to be gone through before quitting the premises is to drink a glass of the very best with that charming old gentleman, who I hope still flourishes amid his bottles and his disgorgers. And when it is added that there are usually upwards of 15,000,000 bottles in the cellars at one time, the old heresy as to the district being unable to supply sufficient wine save for Russian consumption is at once exploded.

In fact some twenty-five millions of gallons of champagne are produced, annually, in the district. Of course not all of it is of the finest growth, and some of it a connoisseur would reject with scorn. In order to smash another old fallacy it is, perhaps, hardly necessary to add that champagne is *not* made from gooseberries—at all events in countries where grapes grow. And the reason for this is that gooseberry juice is far scarcer, and therefore more expensive than grape juice. Some few dozens may be made in England, but to make sufficient gooseberry champagne to be profitable would require more berries than are grown in the country. It would, in fact, require hundreds of tons of the fruit to pay the manufacturer.

Lest my readers should be wearied of the subject of French wines, I shall not particularize as to the burgundies, but confine myself to the clarets of the country which are by far the more popular wines in England—even when they are artificially manufactured, in Spain, and elsewhere.

" The wines that be made in Bordeaux," wrote Gervase Markham, in the middle of the seventeenth century, " are called Gascoyne wines, and you shall know them by their hazel hoopes, and the most be full gadge, and sound wines."

Evidently adulteration's artful aid was but little employed in those days.

"See that in your choice of Gascoine wines," continues Gervase, in his minute direction to the overwrought "housewife," "that your Clarret wines be faire coloured, and bright as a Rubie, not deepe as an Ametist ; for though it may shew strength, yet it wants neatnesse. If your Clarret wine be faint, and have lost his color, then take a fresh hogshead with his fresh lees which was very good wine, and draw your wine into the same, then stop it close and tight, and lay it a foretake for two or three daies that the lees may run through it, then lay it up till it be fine, and if the colour be not perfit, draw it into a red wine hogshead . . . and if your Clarret wine have lost his colour, take a pennyworth of Damsens——" ha ! what is this ?

"Or else blacke Bullesses, as you see cause, and stew them with some red wine of the deepest colour, and make thereof a pound or more of sirrup, and put it into a cleane glasse, and after into the hogshead of Clarret wine ; and the same you may likewise doe unto red wine if you please."

Ahem ! Evidently they did know something about adulteration in the seventeenth century.

It is a common idea that only a very few clarets are entitled to the prefix " Château." The truth is very different. The district on the south bank of the Gironde simply teems with châteaux, of a kind. For miles you cannot go a few hundred yards in any direction without seeing or passing two or three ; each with its vineyards and cellars and special labels, and more or less unblemished reputation. There is Château

Latour, and there is (or may be) the Château
Smith. Did I choose to buy a cottage in that
district, grow my own grapes, and make my own
wines, I should be fully entitled to label them
"Château Gubbins," and incur no penalty by so
doing.

But please do not pick the ripe grapes,
although you may be sorely tempted by the
sight of dozens of bunches separated from the
vines by their sheer weight, and lying in the
furrows. Plenty of people do commit this sort
of theft, for there be hundreds of the rough
element who visit the Médoc country. The
"Hooligans" and *gamins* of Bordeaux drift here
at picking-time just as the poor of London
drift into the county of Kent during the hopping
season. They are not loved, but they have to
be endured. Somebody must pick the grapes,
and after all a few depredations will not ruin the
grower any more than do the strawberry-pickers
in the south of England "break" the growers,
by adopting their usual plan: "three in the
mouth, one in the basket."

The claret-cellars are not nearly as far
beneath the earth as are those in the region
about Rheims. Nor are they as amusing. There
is no "pop, pop" down here, no danger of wounds
and lacerations from flying splinters of glass.
The principal objects of interest are the cobwebs
which are piled up all over the place like dusky
curtains. It is not well to sample too many
glasses which may be offered you of the wine of
the country. For the samples are taken from
the new, immature wine, and are suggestive of

pains and disturbances below the belt. The
head cellarman, portly and urbane like his
brother of Rheims, will watch your face closely
as you taste his novelties, and will invariably ask
your opinion of it. But the wise visitor will
not be too opinionative on the subject. I have
noticed that the man who says the least is
accounted the most knowing, whether he be
inspecting the contents of a cellar, or of a stable.
And believe me, there is as much rubbish talked
about wine as about horses. Still, in sampling
new champagne you may praise indiscriminately,
without being accounted an absolute dunce;
whilst with claret it is altogether different. The
wine varies exceedingly with the vintage; and
none but an expert and accomplished palate may
dare to say what is good, what is bad, and what
is mediocre.

Is it necessary to state that claret was not
drunk, on ordinary occasions, by the Ancient
Britons? I trow not. And I fancy the wines
of the noble old Romans partook more of the
nature of burgundies than clarets. In England
the wines of Médoc have never been fully
appreciated until during the latter half of the
present century, when the taste for port began
to die out, with the good port itself. And as I
writhe, occasionally, in the throes of gout, I
bethink me of the merciless law delivered unto
Moses, which provides that the sins of the
fathers shall be visited upon their descendants,
even unto the third and fourth generation. For
the good old three-and-four-bottle men of eighty
years ago, and farther back than that, certainly laid

the foundations for much of the trouble at this
end of the century. Still there be doctors who
actually recommend port wine as a gout-fuge.
And it is certainly safer to drink a little good
port — matured in the wood, and innocent of
beeswing — an you be a podagric subject, than
some of the clarets which, thanks to the enterprise
of the late Mr. W. E. Gladstone, are within the
reach of the slenderest purse.

Do not smoke whilst drinking claret, or port,
either. Nothing destroys the flavour of red
wine so effectually as the flavour of a cigar.

One of the greatest "sells" ever experienced
by an expectant party of claret judges—of whom
I posed as one—was after this fashion. Our
host had inherited a pipe of Château Lafitte '64,
which had been duly bottled off. We had
enjoyed a nice plain little dinner — a bit of
crimped cod, a steak, and a bird—in order the
better to taste the luscious wine. After dinner
bottle number one made its appearance; and as
they sipped, and prepared to sing hymns of
praise, the jaws of the guests fell. And a great
cry uprose: "Pricked!"

CHAPTER XIII

THE OLD WINES AND THE NEW

Decline and fall of port—Old topers—A youthful wine-bibber—
The whisky age succeeds the port age—" Jeropiga "—Land-
ladies' port—A monopoly—Port *v.* gout—A quaint break-
fast in Reading—About nightcaps—Sherry an absolutely
pure wine—Except when made within the four miles' radius
—Treading the grapes—" Yeso "—Pliny pops up again—
" Lime in the sack " — What the *Lancet* says — " Old
Sherry "—*Faux pas* of a General—About vintages.

On the decline and fall of port wine volumes
might be written. At the same time I am not
the man who is going to write them. According to early recollections, the conversation of
my elders was limited to hunting, racing, and
the wines of Oporto. The man who had "'20,"
or "Comet," port in his cellars was a man to be
cultivated, and dined with ; whilst "'34" and
"'47" men were next in demand. And this
was after the era of the three-and-four-bottle
heroes, of whose deeds I have heard my father
speak, almost with bated breath ; how, after the
retirement of the ladies, to discuss tea and
scandal by themselves, the dining-room door
would be locked by the host himself, who would

pocket the key thereof. Many of the guests
slept where they fell, "repugnant to command,"
like the sword of Pyrrhus ; whilst others would
be fastened in the interior of their chariots at a
later hour. Even in the late fifties, the estimable
divine with whom I was studying the beauties
of the classics, would on the frequent occasion of
a dinner-party provide one bottle of port per
head, for his guests, in addition to hock, champagne, and sherry ; and the writer, then a boy of
fifteen, was included amongst the "heads."

But as the stone age succeeded the ice age, as
the iron age succeeded the stone age, and as the
gold age, and the railway age, and the rotten
company age succeeded the iron age, so have the
whisky age, and the "small bottle" age, and the
gin-and-bitters age almost wiped out the age
when man drank, talked, and thought port. Our
ancestors were immoderate in their potations but,
as far as wine went, these were but rarely indulged
in until after sundown, although the Briton
would frequently wash his breakfast down with
ale of the strongest. And it is difficult to
believe that the evil habit of "nipping," at all
hours of the day, which now prevails in some
circles—a habit which is mainly due to the
break-neck pace at which life is pursued—is
either more conducive to health or intellectuality,
or morality than the after-dinner debauch of a
century ago.

The "hot and heady" wine is (or, rather,
was) produced chiefly in a mountainous district
of Portugal called Cima de Douro. The wine
is largely mixed with spirit even during fermen-

tation, the proper colour being given by a mixture known as *jeropiga*, which is a preparation of elder-berries, molasses, raisin juice, and spirit.

The wine which is made within the Metropolitan Police District, for the special benefit of landladies, infirmaries, and she-choristers, is also treated with a similar mixture, with the addition of a little logwood-extract; but in fashionable quarters the mixture is not known as *jeropiga*, a name which would probably affect the sale.

Port wine was known in England before the year 1700, but was not in much demand. From the year mentioned till 1826 the export trade was a monopoly in the hands of English merchants. The effect of this monopoly was to increase the price in England, and to gradually deteriorate the quality. Exports from Oporto have decreased in a marked way for the last forty years or so; and although there is still some demand, and some decent wine left, the "hot and heady" concoction whether dry or fruity, a lady's wine, or a military ditto, is gradually leaving us.

The pity of it! And simultaneously with its departure comes the pronouncement of the medical profession that port (with the exception of the "old crusted" brand) does *not* encourage gout to abide within the human frame. I may fairly claim to have been a "port man" all my life, and never, when serving Her Majesty, overlooked my orthodox allowance of the "black strap" purchased with the Prince Regent's allowance. Nevertheless I am not going to recommend this description of wine as an ideal breakfast drink; although very early in life I once made trial of it at nine o'clock one morning.

This was in the good town of Reading, in company with a schoolmate or two. We were on our way home for the holidays, and had been entrusted, for the first part of the journey, to the care of the French master. Him we had evaded for the time being—he was much interested in the manufacture of sweet biscuits—and marching boldly into the best inn's best room, we demanded bread and cheese and a bottle of the most expensive port on the wine-list. Schoolboy-like our fancy turned to quaintness in the matter of meals ; and I am bound to add that the state of our health was not one whit improved by this weird breakfast. As for the French master, no sooner had he run us to earth, than—— but that part of the story is too painful to tell.

One of the oldest winter beverages known to civilization is

Bishop,

a composition of port wine and spices of which it has been written :—

> Three cups of this a prudent man may take ;
> The first of these for constitution's sake,
> The second to the girl he loves the best,
> The third and last to lull him to his rest.

And an effectual luller is this Bishop.

Make several incisions in the rind of a lemon, stick cloves in the incisions, and roast the lemon at a slow fire. Put small but equal quantities of cinnamon, cloves, mace, and all-spice into a sauce-pan, with half a pint of water ; let it boil until reduced one-half. Boil one bottle of port wine ; burn a portion of the spirit out of it by applying a lighted paper to the saucepan. Put the roasted lemon and spice into the wine, stir it well, and let it stand near the fire ten minutes. Rub a few lumps of sugar on the rind of a lemon, put the sugar into a bowl with the juice of half a lemon (not roasted), pour the wine into it, grate some nutmeg into it, sweeten to taste, and serve with the lemon and spices floating on the surface.

To sum up, the decline and fall of port in British estimation may be said to be due, mainly, to the following causes : inferiority of most of the modern vintages, the introduction of whisky, the present taste for lighter wines, such as the cheaper clarets and burgundies, with the wines of Germany and Italy, and a sort of " boom " in wines from Australia and California.   These last-named, however, are but seldom seen at the tables of the wealthy ; and thus far the demand for the productions of gallant little Wales have not been in any great request, although the demand is said to be equal to the supply.

Sherry, the " sack " which was said to cheer the heart of Sir John Falstaff and other of Shake-speare's heroes, is, like port, a light of other days. Like the wine of Portugal, also, its exportation has for many years been in the hands of English settlers. The following startling statistics have been published about these exports, which statistics speak for themselves : The output to England in 1891 was 2,135,969 gallons, or *sixty-four per*

cent less than in 1873, which was the "record"
sherry year. And although many efforts have
been made to stem the ebb, the last seven
years have shewn a steady decrease in the
exports.

Yet, according to the best authorities, sherry
is not only the purest, but the most wholesome of
all wines. Of course, in making this statement
the wine of Spain, the *vino de Jerez* is implied,
and not the home-made productions for the malefit of those who study economy without due
regard to digestion. Strictly speaking, sherry
means Jerez (pronounced "herreth") wine. But
Manzanilla, a wine which is made at St. Lucas,
and Montilla which comes from a town south of
Cordova, may come under the same category.
And with a view of shewing the wholesomeness
of sherry it is stated, by no less an authority than
the *Lancet*, that it is the only wine enjoined in
the preparations of the wines of the British
Pharmacopœia, with two exceptions—viz. *vinum
ferri citratis*, and *vinum quininae*, which are made
with orange wine. Therefore it is certain that
the sufferer from gout, for whom *vinum colchici*
is prescribed, may swallow a proportion of the
juice of the grape, and, possibly, a hair of the
dog which bit him. This naturally recalls the
old story of the sherry which was sent to a former
Lord Chesterfield as a *panacea* for his ailment,
and the curt reply sent : "Sir, I have tried your
sherry, and prefer the gout."

There are several types of sherries, according
to the different characters developed. These are
known by several distinguishing terms compre-

hending the characters and specific qualities of
the wine from one end to the other of a scale
ranging from delicate and light wines to rich,
generous, and dark-coloured wines.   Between a
straw-coloured *Vino de Pasto* and the very fine
Old East India Brown—the sherry which two
decades ago was in enormous demand at such old-
fashioned hostelries as the "Rainbow" in Fleet
Street, ere the reign of gin-and-bitters—there is
a vast difference, both in colour and flavour.
Broadly, however, sherry may be divided into
two classes—*fino*, a light-coloured, delicate light
wine of the Amontillado type, and the *oloroso*, a
full-bodied, highly-developed wine.

The sherry grapes are collected and placed in
large panniers on the backs of mules and conveyed to the press-houses.   The press is of very
primitive construction, and is identical with those
used in ancient history.   It consists simply of a
wooden trough about ten feet square, provided in
the centre with a screw press, which is used after
the treading by foot power is done, to get the
last drop of juice out of the crushed mass.
Rather less than a ton of grapes serves for one
pressing, and the idea that this is done with the
naked feet of the Spanish peasantry is a popular
error.   Sherry is not kneaded like German bread.
Men clad in light clothing and shod with wooden
clogs, with nails on the soles and heels, pointing
in a slanting direction, proceed to tread the
grapes in a most methodical manner, proceeding
row by row, each row being of the width of the
nailed sole of the clog.

After the grapes have been trodden over for

the first time, *i.e.* partly crushed and bruised, a measured quantity of sulphate of lime (*Yeso*) is sprinkled over the sticky mass—now I have gone so far perhaps 'twould be as well to complete the narrative, although it is not always wise to enquire too closely into the interior economy of wine presses, or kitchens. This sulphate of lime is a pure native earth, found in the neighbourhood of Jerez, and is burnt before being mixed with the grapes. How many sherry drinkers, I wonder, know how largely mother earth enters into their pet tipple? The idea, certainly, does not seem a nice one, but this mixing of lime with sherry is a very ancient custom indeed.

Pliny—where should we modern bookmakers be without dear old Pliny?—mentions the custom as an ancient African one. And in days of yore it must be remembered that Africa was not entirely populated by cannibals and dervishes, but was the home of many who lived wisely and well.

" There's lime in the sack ! " is a sentence put into the mouth of Falstaff. In modern days the process has become known as " plastering," from the fact that plaster-of-Paris consists principally of sulphate of lime or burnt gypsum.

" It is interesting," says the *Lancet*, " to surmise the origin of this very ancient custom. That it had some intelligent basis admits of no doubt. Some think that it had its origin in the fact being noticed that when the grape juice was fermented in alabaster vessels or in marble tanks the wine was better, it clarified quicker, and developed character more satisfactorily. Others regard the addition of sulphate of lime as convenient from a mechanical point of view during the pressing ; it was necessary when the grapes were wetter than usual in order to bind the residuary mass together. We do not incline to this view."

As the *Lancet* devotes a considerable space to the exposition of the view to which it does incline I may be excused from quoting it in full —more especially as there be tables of percentages, and complicated mathematical calculations in said exposition. But it is proved to the satisfaction of the *Lancet* that " lime in the sack " is matter in the right place. And although to an unedu-cated mind lime suggests such terrifying develop-ments of *tarda podagra* as chalk-stones, possibly the action of the grapes on the lime renders it innocuous.

It is a curious fact that sherry in keeping develops a slight increase of alcohol as the time advances. All spirit added to sherry, however, is obtained from wine itself, corn-spirit in Spain being quite a superfluity, since wine-spirit can be produced so cheaply and in unlimited quantity. Moreover the importation of German spirit into Spain is made practically impossible by a pro-hibitive duty. Still, unless rumour lies, some Spanish wines receive the German spirit after exportation ; so Spain " gets there just the same."

Here is an item of news which should inspire confidence in the sceptic.

" Good brandy—*i.e.* a genuine wine-distilled

L

spirit—is being produced in Spain in commercial quantities which it is to be hoped will successfully compete with the stuff erroneously called brandy, not to say Cognac, but of which not a drop has been derived from the grape."

In my researches into the manufacture of port and sherry, I have come across no mention of the phylloxera. I am, therefore, halting between the beliefs, either that the Spaniards and Portuguese understand vermin better than do the French, or that the "vine-louse" has her own reasons for keeping out of Spain and Portugal.

Forty years ago an estimable Irish nobleman was known as "Old Sherry," from his partiality to that wine. And thirty years ago I was once seated at the table of a General of Division, up at Simla. My right-hand neighbour was a son of this same nobleman, but our host, apparently, did not know this—or had forgotten the fact. At all events, during a lull in the conversation, the General (who had a voice like sharpening a saw) rapped out : " By the way, Captains—you say you've been quartered in Ireland—did you ever meet ' Old Sherry ' there ? "

A subaltern can't very well throw a dinner-roll at a General or stick a carving-fork into his leg ; but that is what I, personally, felt like doing.

In mediæval times a sufficient quantity of wine for the needs of the inhabitants was made in gallant little Wales ; and the idea of reviving the industry occurred to the Marquis of Bute, who has done so much for the welfare of Cardiff and the neighbourhood. The vineyards are on the site of the old ones, facing south, and the vines were planted twenty years ago, and are very hardy. There is no reason why they should not be propagated to almost any extent, and there is abundant scope for the extension of the vineyards and a proportionate increase in the yield of wine.

The vintages of 1885, 1890, and 1891 are marked in Messrs. Hatch, Mansfield and Co.'s list as " All sold," and although the vintage of '98, owing to the long spell of dry weather, does not promise particularly well, the Marquis is no more unfortunate in this respect than most other vine-growers.

Vintages.

As my readers may not all be connoisseurs in the matter of wines, a few words on the subject of vintages may be appropriate, at the close of this chapter.

With regard to champagnes, the good years are '65, '68, '74 (especially good), '78, '80, '84, '85, '87 (somewhat light in body), '89, '92, and '93. All the other vintages since '65 have turned out more or less badly ; and there have been no good vintages since '93.

One of the largest and best vintages of claret on record is that of '75, which ranks with the older ones of '48, '58, and '64. '77 is fair, and between that year and '88 there was no vintage of particular merit. '93 wine is good, and this year furnished the largest yield since '75. '94 wine is exceptionally bad. During the five years from '82 to '86 the merits of the wines were completely destroyed by mildew.

The burgundy vintages have been good since '84. As for ports, the drinkable wines (since '34) are those of '41, '47 (one of the finest wines ever known), '51 (exceptionally good), '52, '53 (fine and fruity), '54, '58, '63, '68, '70, '72, '75, '78 (exceptionally fine), '81, '84, ' 87 (the best since '78), and '96 which "shews promise." The worst years are '55, '56, '57, '59, '64, '66, '69, '71, '74, '76, '77, '79, '80, '82, '83, '86, '88, '91, '93 (exceptionally bad), '94, and '95.

The above statistics are also from Messrs. Hatch, Mansfield and Co.'s list.

CHAPTER XIV

THE LONG AND THE SHORT OF IT

The Long Drink—Cremorne Gardens—Hatfield—Assorted cocktails—Brandy-and-Soda—Otherwise Stone Fence—Bull's
milk—A burglar's brew—More cocktails—A "swizzle"—
L'Amour Poussée—A corpse reviver—A golden slipper—A
heap of comfort.

OUR grandfathers knew not the Long Drink ;
the chief reason for this fact being that aërated
water, and consequently large tumblers, had not
been invented. And soda-water—one of the most
ineffectual restoratives I know—was originally
employed, under its pet name "sober water," as
a pick-me-up. The Long Drink came in, I
fancy, with Cremorne. At primæval Vauxhall
men still refreshed themselves with glasses of
alleged sherry, and with rummers of brandy-and-
water—a flat, stale, and unprofitable potion, which
nobody who is in complete possession of his
faculties thinks of imbibing nowadays.

Let us now run over a few recipes which
require large tumblers to hold the drinks. And
we will commence with " cobblers," those seductive warm-weather importations from the United
States.

Catawba Cobbler,

so called because Catawba (which is a Californian wine and but little known in this island of ours) is seldom used in its concoction. Champagne is an excellent substitute, whilst a cheaper one is the Italian wine, sparkling Asti.

Dissolve one teaspoonful of sifted sugar in one tablespoonful of water in a tumbler ; add two glasses of Catawba, or Asti, or champagne, and fill the tumbler with crushed ice. Shake, ornament with a slice of orange or pine-apple, and drink through straws.

Moselle Cobbler.

One glass of sparkling moselle in a large tumbler, a spot of old brandy, sugar to taste, a slice of lemon, and filled up with crushed ice.

But there is a sameness in the manufacture of cobblers, in which almost every known wine, or strong water, may be used, with the other ingredients, ice, sugar, slices of lemon or orange, and water (not much water) added.

"The secret of making

" Hatfield,"

writes an invaluable authority, "is supposed to be a secret only known to the manager at The Oval. We used to drink at the Old Winchester Music Hall an imitation, composed of two bottles of soda-water to one ginger-beer, a quartern of Old Tom and a half-quartern of noyeau, duly iced."

Most "cocktails" come under the heading of

"Short Drinks," and will be found duly scheduled, farther on. Here, however, is a long 'un.

Saratoga Cocktail.

Put into a large tumbler twenty drops of pineapple syrup, twelve of Angostura bitters, twenty of maraschino, and a wine-glass of old brandy; nearly fill the glass with pounded ice, and mix well. Add two or three strawberries and a shred of thin lemon-peel, and top up with champagne.

Arctic Regions.

Large tumbler. Quarter of a pint of milk, wineglass of sherry, and liqueur-glass of old brandy. Fill up with pounded ice, and sweeten to taste. Shake well, dust with cinnamon, and suck through a straw.

Brandy-and-Soda.

Every Saturday morning, of all respectable newsagents, in the pink paper, price——— Pshaw! What am I thinking about? This concoction is also known in America as "Stone Wall" (Why?), and used to be known in Her Majesty's dominions in Asia as a "Peg"—simply because every dose swallowed was said to represent a peg in the coffin being manufactured for the swallower. It is unnecessary to give any recipe for this mixture, the proportion of the ingredients varying with the inclination, disposition, indisposition, state of health, or pocket, of the swallower. But above all let your ingredients be of the best. There is only one thing worse than bad brandy, and that is bad soda-water. Avoid the cheap stuff with the little glass stoppers, as you would the tipstaff.

Brandy Daisy.

Put into a large tumbler the juice of a small lemon, half a tablespoonful of sifted sugar, and dissolve with one squirt of aërated water from a syphon. Add a liqueur-glass of yellow chartreuse, nearly fill the glass with crushed ice, and add one wine-glassful of old brandy. Stir well and strain.

Bull's Milk

A large tumbler. One teaspoonful of sifted sugar, half a pint of milk, one-third of a wine-glassful of old rum, one wine-glassful of old brandy. Add ice, shake, strain into another glass, and dust with cinnamon and nutmeg.

Julap, or Julep.

Behold this cordial Julap here,
That flames and dances in his crystal bounds,
With spirits of balm and fragrant syrups mixt.

Although the mint julep is compounded and used principally in the continent of America, the original " julap " is a Persian word, signifying a sweet potion. John Quincey, the author of a dictionary on Physic, describes julap as "an extemporaneous form of medicine, made of simple and compound water, sweetened, and serves for a vehicle to other forms not so convenient to take alone."

The simple water is usually omitted nowadays. And here is one recipe for a Mint Julep.

Pound a quantity of ice quite fine, enough to half fill a large tumbler. Add two teaspoonfuls of sugar. Then add a wine-glass of old brandy, half a wine-glass of old rum, and two or three sprigs of mint. Stir well together, and drink through a straw.

Another way to make a

Mint Julep.

Put into a large tumbler two and a half tablespoonfuls of water, a tablespoonful of sugar, and two or three sprigs of mint pressed well into the sugar-and-water to extract the flavour; add one and a half wine-glassfuls of brandy, fill up with crushed ice, shake well, draw the sprigs of mint to the top of the glass with the stems downwards, and decorate with berries in season and small slices of orange; dust with a little sugar, and dash with rum. Serve with a straw.

Mint julep, it may be added, is supposed to have been introduced into England by Captain Marryat, the nautical novelist.

Pine-apple Julep.

This is a beverage for bookmakers and company-promoters only. All others should substitute pine-apple syrup from the tin for the slice of pine-apple.

Large tumbler. Slice of pine-apple. The juice of half an orange, ten drops of maraschino, ten drops

of raspberry syrup, half a wine-glassful of gin ; half
fill the tumbler with crushed ice, shake well, and
top up with champagne.   Drink through straws.

Saratoga Brace-up.

Large tumbler, tablespoonful sifted sugar, twelve
drops of Angostura bitters, twelve drops of lemon
juice, six drops of lime juice, twelve drops of
anisette, one fresh egg, and a wine-glass of old
brandy.   Half fill the glass with crushed ice, shake
thoroughly, strain into another large tumbler, and
fill up with Seltzer or Apollinaris water.

A Burglar's Brew.

Amongst the kind and generous correspondents
who have furnished me with matter for this
work is an Austrian gentleman, who, apparently,
holds some appointment under Government.   He
writes : "Our local man in blue (or rather in
green, in Prussia) and I have just driven twenty
miles a burglar to the police-station.   Bobby
and I being both new to this part of the world,
did not know the road, but our passenger directed
us quite well, and actually rang the bell himself
at the gaol ; after which he most properly wished
a very happy new year to the head constable,
with whom he seemed to be quite on sitting
terms.

"But the point of this is to tell you of a very
decent drink, mixed by 'Billy'"—presumably
the burglar—"himself, on our journey—a most
acceptable 'gargle,' with two feet of snow and a
beastly east wind.

" 2 pints lager beer, brought to boiling point.
3 glass rhum.
3 glass cognac.
8 lumps sugar.
1 lemon.

" I am afraid the poor fellow won't get another taste of it for five years."

Lager beer and " rhum " does not read particularly delectable. But there is no accounting for tastes ; and possibly the Burglar's Brew may find favour amongst some of my young friends.

Reserving the right to re-enter upon the subject of long drinks, I will now touch upon a short one or two. *Imprimis,*

Cocktails,

another brand of beverages which our American cousins have introduced into the old country. I am bound to add that the beverage in question has not altogether " frozen on " here, although the American Bar has become an institution in all fashionable and much - frequented quarters. In the land of its birth the cocktail is said to be popular at shooting or fishing parties. But on this side the host who wants his guests to shoot straight does not ply them freely with fancy drinks.

Brandy Cocktail.

To save wearisome repetition of words, it should be stated at the outset that the cocktail is almost invariably mixed in a small tumbler, in which the necessary crushed ice has been placed first.

One wine-glass of brandy, thirty drops of gum syrup, six drops of Angostura bitters, and twenty drops of curaçoa. Stir, and shake well. Place a small shred of lemon-peel atop.

Champagne Cocktail.

One teaspoonful of sugar, ten drops of Angostura bitters, a slice of pine-apple, and a small shred of lemon-peel. Fill up with champagne, mix, and strain.

Coomassie Cocktail.

Break the yolk of an egg into the tumbler, and mix with it a teaspoonful of sugar ; add six drops of Angostura bitters, a small wine-glass of sherry, and one-third of a glass of brandy. Shake and strain ; then dust with nutmeg and cinnamon.

Jersey Cocktail.

Instead of crushed ice, put two nice little blocks in the tumbler, add one teaspoonful of sugar, one teaspoonful of orange bitters, and half a wine-glass of old brandy. Top up with bottled cider, and mix with a spoon. Serve with a strawberry and a sprig of verbena atop.

Manhattan Cocktail.

Half a wine-glass of Italian vermouth, half a wine-glass of rye whisky, ten drops of Angostura bitters, and ten drops of curaçoa. Shake and strain, and place a small shred of lemon-peel atop.

Bengal Cocktail.

Thirty drops of maraschino, one teaspoonful of pine-apple syrup, thirty drops of curaçoa, six drops of Angostura bitters, one wine-glass of old brandy. Mix, etc., and add peel.

Newport Cocktail.

Two *lumps* of ice, and a small *slice* of lemon in the tumbler, add six drops of Angostura, half a wine-glass of noyeau, and a wine-glass of brandy. Mix, etc., and add peel.

Gin Cocktail.

Thirty drops of gum syrup, ten drops of Angostura, one wine-glass of gin, ten drops of curaçoa. Mix, etc., and add peel.

A " Swizzle,"

which is well known in fashionable circles as a morning "livener," somewhat resembles the above concoction, but is even more seductive and enthralling. When I gave the recipe for this in *Cakes and Ale*, it brought down upon my devoted head the horror and indignation of many of the good young critics of the superior dailies. Yet the swallow is harmless enough, absolutely innocuous — save to the melancholy vapours. And to shew my utter lack of appreciation of friendly warnings I append the same recipe in all its original beauty :—

Crushed ice (this is a welcome addition), a wine-glassful of Hollands, a liqueur-glassful of curaçoa, three drops of Angostura, a little sugar, and half a small bottle of Seltzer water. Churn up the mixture with a swizzle-stick, which can be easily made with the assistance of a short length of cane (the ordinary school-treat brand), a piece of cork, a bit of string, and a pocket-knife.

Martini Cocktail.

Thirty drops of gum syrup, thirty drops of orange bitters, half a wine-glass of gin, and half a wine-glass of vermouth ; fill with crushed ice, shake, strain, and place a small piece of lemon-peel atop.

Sherry Cocktail

is made in the same way as the above, leaving out the gin and vermouth, and substituting a wine-glass of sherry.

Sunrise Cocktail

Thirty drops of vanilla syrup, ten drops of Angostura, two-thirds of a wine-glass of sherry and one-third of a wine-glass of brandy ; mix, strain, and add peel.

Jockey-Club Cocktail

(although it may seem high-treason to connect the Jockey Club with a cocktail).

Thirty drops of gum syrup, ten drops of Angostura, ten drops of raspberry syrup, half a wine-glass of gin, and half a wine-glass of vermouth ; shake, strain, and add peel.

Whisky Cocktail

is made in the same way as the above, omitting the raspberry syrup, gin, and vermouth ; and this brings us to the end of cocktails.

There is a fancy drink which is known in different parts of the world under different names, and some of the ingredients in which differ slightly. In the Mediterranean islands it is known as a

Knickerbein,

and this is the way to make it.

Break into a small tumbler the yolk of one egg, add one-third of a wine-glass of curaçoa, one-third of a wine-glass of maraschino, and one-third of a wine-glass of brandy ; add pounded ice, shake well, and strain ; whisk the white of an egg to a stiff froth, and place it on the top ; dust with pink sugar, and suck through a straw.

In France there is a somewhat similar potion known as

L'Amour Poussée,

which also figures under other names in different parts of the great continent of America, and in the West Indies.

Take a spiral glass (see that you get this) and fill it one-third full of maraschino ; place carefully in it the unbeaten yolk of an egg. Surround this with syrup of vanilla, and fill up the glass with old brandy. These ingredients *must not mix;* and in order to prevent this, pour them over the back of the bowl of a teaspoon into the glass.

Brandy Scaffa

sounds Amur'can, and is. Here again the ingredients must not be allowed to commingle, and the egg-yolk is omitted.

A quarter of a glass of raspberry syrup, into a spiral glass, and a like amount of maraschino and green chartreuse. Fill up—I always make this in an old-fashioned champagne-glass, and generally omit the raspberry syrup—with the best old brandy you can get.

Corpse Reviver

is the same sort of drink, with some difference in the ingredients.

A spiral glass, filled with one-third maraschino, one-third brandy, and one-third curaçoa.

If the corpse came my way and I loved it, I should leave out the maraschino. In

Golden Slipper

the egg-yolk reappears.

Place the yolk of an egg in a spiral wine-glass, half full of yellow chartreuse. Fill up with Dantzicer goldwasser, and do not let the ingredients mix. This goldwasser is said to be the oldest liqueur known in Europe, having been introduced into France by the Italians in the time of Catharine de Medici. Its origin is undoubtedly Italian, and the colourless liquor made in Dantzic, with the fragments of gold leaf floating therein, is a fiery imitation of the real thing.

One more short recipe to finish this chapter.

Heap of Comfort.

Put into a small tumbler the yolk of one egg, two-thirds of a wine-glass of sherry, one-third of a wine-glass of brandy, ten drops of curaçoa, and a teaspoonful of sugar. Add pounded ice, shake well, and strain into a coloured claret-glass. Dust over with nutmeg.

M

CHAPTER XV

"SANGAREE" is generally associated with soft-
shell crabs and "yellow Jack"; nevertheless
here are a few recipes for concocting the drink,
in its various forms.

Ale Sangaree.

Put into a large tumbler a teaspoonful of sifted
sugar, and a tablespoonful of water to dissolve it.
Add a small lump of ice, and fill up with a mixture
of bitter and Burton ales. Dust with nutmeg.
This drink may also be served hot, *without* the ice;
need it be added?

Brandy Sangaree.

Put into a small tumbler one teaspoonful of
sugar, half a wine-glassful of water, one wine-glassful

of brandy, and fill up with crushed ice.   Mix with
a spoon, dash the top with port wine, and grated
nutmeg.

Gin Sangaree

is made in exactly the same way, substituting
Old Tom for brandy.

Port Wine Sangaree.

A small tumbler, a glass and a half of port, and
a teaspoonful of sugar.   Add crushed ice, shake
well, strain into another glass, and dust with
nutmeg.

Porteree

is made like ale sangaree, with the substitution
of porter for ale.   And in

Sherry Sangaree

the wine of Spain takes the place of the wine of
Portugal.

Slings

can be made with brandy, gin, or whisky.   The
Americans mix a wine-glassful of the spirit with
half a wine-glassful of water, a teaspoonful of
sifted sugar, and a lump of ice.   In England
soda-water is mixed with the spirit.   What we
call a gin-sling is known in the United States
as a

John Collins,

but in certain regimental messes this "John"
used not to be considered properly attired without

the addition of a little curaçoa—the quantity
varying with the effect it was intended to produce
upon the unsuspecting guest.   Occasionally, at
about sunrise, boiling water was substituted for
soda-water.

Brandy Smash.

Put into a small tumbler half a tablespoonful of
sifted sugar, one tablespoonful of water and a wine-
glassful of old brandy ; add crushed ice, and shake
well.   Put in a sprig or two of mint, with two slices
of orange on the top, and drink through a straw.

Champagne Smash.

Small tumbler, tablespoonful of sugar ; ice, and
fill up with champagne.   Add mint, as in above
recipe, and serve with a straw.

Gin Smash.

Small tumbler, teaspoonful of sugar, half a wine-
glassful of water, and a wine-glassful of gin.   Add
ice, mint, and a slice or two of orange.   Serve with
a straw.

Whisky Smash

is made in the same way, substituting whisky
(Irish or Scotch) for gin.

Santa Cruz Smash.

Put into a small tumbler one teaspoonful of
sugar, half a wine-glassful of water, and a wine-
glassful of Santa Cruz, or white rum.   Add crushed
ice, and mint.   Serve with a straw.

Apple Jack Sour

is but seldom called for in this tight little island.

In America it is made in a large tumbler, with half a tablespoonful of sugar, the juice of half a lemon, a squirt of Seltzer water from a syphon, and a wine-glassful of old cider brandy. Nearly fill the glass with crushed ice, and ornament with any fruit in season.

Bourbon Sour.

Small tumbler, one teaspoonful of sugar, the juice and rind of a quarter of a lemon, one wine-glassful of Bourbon whisky. Add crushed ice, shake well, and strain.

Brandy Sour

is exactly the same potion, with the substitution of brandy for Bourbon whisky. And

Whisky Sour

is the same, made with whisky.

At the Bengal Club, Calcutta, the

Gin Sour

has attained to renown.

A large tumbler is used, the juice of six limes is squeezed therein, care being taken to remove the pips. A wine-glassful of Old Tom is added, then a liqueur-glassful of raspberry syrup, three quarters of a liqueur-glassful of orange bitters, a wine-glassful of water, and three drops of Angostura bitters. Nearly fill the tumbler with crushed ice, and shake.

Sherry Sour.

Put into a small tumbler one teaspoonful of sugar, the juice and rind of a quarter of a lemon, one wineglassful of sherry, and nearly fill the tumbler with crushed ice. Shake, strain, and dash with strawberry syrup.

Home Ruler

was a favourite drink at the bars of the House of Commons, during the reign of the Uncrowned King.

The yolks of two eggs, well beaten, were placed in a large tumbler, a little sifted sugar was added, and a small tumblerful of hot milk was gradually stirred into the mixture. Last of all a large wineglassful of " John Jameson " was added.

A curious recipe comes from Switzerland, an elaborate method of

Burning Brandy,

or any other spirit but gin.

Cut the top off a lemon, and hollow out the interior with the handle-end of a spoon. Place the empty cone thus formed by the skin on the top of a large wine-glass. Fill the cone with brandy, rum, or whisky ; take a fork, balance a piece of sugar on the prongs, set the spirit alight, and hold the sugar over the flame until it has melted into the cone. Then take a skewer, and pierce a small hole in the base of the cone. When all the spirit has trickled into the glass, throw the cone away, and drink the result.

"This process," says my informant, writing from Davos, "sanctifies good liquor, and makes inferior ditto distinctly welcome."

A

Prairie Oyster

serves as a valuable restorative of vital power. The origin of this popular pick-me-up is said to be as follows :—

"Some years since three men were encamped on Texas Prairie, 500 miles from the sea-coast, when one of them was sick unto death with fever, and was frantically crying out for oysters ; he was quite sure that if he could only have an oyster or two he would be cured. After much thought as to how they were to procure what he wanted, one of them, having procured some prairie hens' eggs, not far from the camp, broke one, and putting the yolk into a glass, sprinkled it with a little salt and pepper, adding a little vinegar, and gave it to his sick companion, who declared it was just the thing he wanted ; and from that hour he began to get better, and eventually got quite well."

Turkey Oyster

is the yolk of a turkey's egg treated after the above fashion, and is said to be "greatly in vogue with athletes." But if the athlete be wise he will not omit to swallow the *white* of the egg as well.

The name "negus" is suggestive of a children's party—as well as of the east coast of

Africa; 'tis a comparatively harmless beverage, said to have been invented by one Colonel Negus.

Port Wine Negus.

Put a pint of port wine into a jug, and rub a quarter of a pound of sugar, in lumps, on the rind of a lemon; then squeeze the juice of the lemon and strain it, adding the sugar and lemon juice to the port wine, with a little grated nutmeg. Add to this a quart of boiling water, cover the jug, and when cool the beverage will be fit for use.

Sherry Negus

is made with an extra quarter of a pound of sugar; and a wine-glassful of noyeau or mara-schino may be added.

Egg Nogg

is a bile-raiser, which is made in a large tumbler, and therefore comes under the heading of " Long Drinks."

Beat up an egg with a tablespoonful of sifted sugar; add one tablespoonful of boiling water, one wine-glassful of brandy, and one wine-glassful of rum. Fill up the tumbler with boiling milk, mix well, and dust with nutmeg.

Sherry Egg Nogg

One egg beaten up with a tablespoonful of sugar in a large tumbler, two glasses of sherry; fill up with boiling milk, mix, and dust with nutmeg.

" In another place," I gave the recipe for

A Doctor,

which is a cold edition of the above, and may also be made with brandy or whisky.   In

A Surgeon-Major,

which is a still more valuable—and more expensive —restorative, two eggs are used, and the tumbler is filled up with the choicest brand of champagne kept on the premises.

Blue Blazer

is a " grateful, comforting " drink in cold weather. And it is advisable that the nerves of the mixer be in thoroughly good order, and that he (or she) be steady of hand.

Put into a silver cup, which has been previously heated, a wine-glassful of Scotch whisky (proof) and one wine-glassful of boiling water ; set on fire, and have ready another cup, also heated, and pass the blazing liquid from one cup to the other, three or four times.   Serve in a small tumbler with a little sugar and lemon.

If a good dispensing chemist be within easy reach, the searcher after the hidden truth may try a

Locomotive.

Beat two eggs with a little honey in a jug, add a pinch of ground cloves and a liqueur-glass of curaçoa ; then add, beating all the time, one pint of burgundy made boiling hot.   Dust with nutmeg.

Rumfustian.

Beat up in a large tumbler or jug the yolks of two eggs, with a tablespoonful of sugar ; then take half a pint of Burton ale, one wine-glassful of gin, one wine-glassful of sherry, a little spice, and the rind of a quarter of a lemon. Let the ale, wine, and gin, mixed together, come to the boil, then pour into the egg mixture, whisking rapidly ; serve hot, with a dash of nutmeg atop.

Pope

is a compound of burgundy and brandy (not too much brandy, please) with a little sugar added, poured over two Seville oranges, roasted and cut into quarters. The mixture is then boiled and strained. But, personally, I am not partial to this pope, which is even nastier when made with champagne.

Bull's Milk.

Put into a large tumbler one teaspoonful of icing-sugar, with half a pint of milk, one-third of a wine-glassful of rum, and two-thirds of a wine-glassful of brandy ; add crushed ice, shake well, strain into another glass, and dust with cinnamon and nutmeg.

Brandy Champirelle

is another importation from the land of the stars and stripes.

Take a small tumbler and bestow therein one wine-glassful of brandy, six drops of Angostura bitters, a liqueur-glassful of curaçoa, and some crushed ice. Shake well, and strain.

Black Stripe.

Mix in a small tumbler one wine-glassful of
Santa Cruz, or white rum, one tablespoonful of
golden syrup, and one tablespoonful of water; fill
the tumbler with crushed ice, and shake well.   For
a winter drink, substitute boiling water for ice, and
grate a little nutmeg atop.

Bosom Caresser.

Small tumbler, one wine-glassful of sherry, half
a wine-glassful of brandy, the yolk of an egg, two
teaspoonfuls of sugar, and two grains of cayenne
pepper.   Add ice, shake well, strain, and dust with
nutmeg and cinnamon.

Colleen Bawn.

Small tumbler, one egg beaten with a teaspoonful
of sugar, one-third of a wine-glassful of yellow
chartreuse, and like quantities, respectively, of
benedictine and rye whisky; shake well, strain, and
dust with cinnamon, nutmeg, and pink sugar.

Although the word "Posset" suggests a bad
cold in the head it may be noticed *en route*, with
other potions.   It is a medicated drink of some
antiquity; for among the numerous English
authors who in some way or other speak of it,
the divine William has made one of his characters
say: "We'll have a posset . . . at the latter
end of a sea-coal fire."

And Sir John Suckling, who died in 1641,
says in one of his poems:—

In came the bridesmaids with the posset.

Dr. Johnson describes posset as milk curdled with wine and other acids ; we may therefore infer that the preparation of sherry and curd which we call

White Wine Whey

is the Milk Posset of our ancestors.

Put one pint of milk into a saucepan, and when it boils pour in a gill of sherry ; boil it till the curd becomes hard, then strain it through a fine sieve. Rub a few lumps of sugar on the rind of a lemon and put them into the whey ; grate a small quantity of nutmeg into it, and sweeten to taste.

Pepper Posset.

The better to promote perspiration, whole peppercorns are sometimes boiled in the whey. A Pepper Posset was known to the learned and ingenious John Dryden, as will appear from the following lines written by him :—

A sparing diet did her health assure ;
Or sick, a pepper posset was her cure.

Cider Posset.

Pound the peel of a lemon in a mortar, and pour on it one quart of fresh-drawn cider ; sweeten with lump-sugar, add one gill of brandy and one quart of new milk. Stir the mixture well, strain it through a hair sieve, grate a little nutmeg over it, and it is fit for use.

In a former chapter a recipe for

Sack Posset

has been given.   And here is what Sir Fleetwood
Fletcher wrote on the same subject :—

From fam'd Barbadoes, on the western main,
Fetch sugar, ounces four ; fetch sack from Spain
A pint ; and from the Eastern Indian coast
Nutmeg, the glory of our northern toast ;
O'er flaming coals let them together heat
Till the all-conquering sack dissolve the sweet ;
O'er such another fire put eggs just ten,
New-born from tread of cock and rump of hen ;
Stir them with steady hand and conscience pricking,
To see th' untimely end of ten fine chicken :
      [Sir Fleetwood ! Sir Fleetwood !]

From shining shelf take down the brazen skillet,
A quart of milk from gentle cow will fill it ;
When boil'd and cold, put milk and sack to eggs,
Unite them firmly like the triple league,
        [What, again ?]

And on the fire let them together dwell
Till miss sing twice—you must not kiss and tell :
Each lad and lass take up a silver spoon,
And fall on fiercely like a starv'd dragoon.

CHAPTER XVI

" APPLE SASS "

ACCORDING to some chroniclers the ancient
Britons made cider — or " seider " as the poor
ignoramuses wrote it—but it must have been nasty
stuff, according to our civilized ideas ; for until
the Romans came to visit us the apple was not
cultivated in Britain, nor, indeed, any fruit or
vegetable. Our blue forefathers were not particular as to what they ate or drank ; and I
should think the fermented juice of wild or
" crab " apples must have corroded the throats
of the hardiest.

It is claimed for cider, and perry, that no
fermented drinks do less hurt to the imbiber ;
although one authority states that the man who

drinks too much of either invariably falls on the back of his head, which sounds rather dangerous. Whether the drinking of cider in moderation conduces to long life deponent sayeth not ; but no less an authority than Lord Bacon evidently thought so ; and in his *History of Life and Death* he tells of eight men dancing a Morris-dance, whose ages, added together, were 800 years, " tennants of one Mannour " belonging to the Earl of Essex, and habitual cider-drinkers. But the lengthening of the days of the imbiber depends, in all probability, upon the brand of cider. I have tasted some varieties which were capable, apparently, of shortening life, rather than of prolonging it ; and in parts of Somersetshire, even at the present day, the locals—case-hardened and poison-proof to a man—swill a horrible decoction, which would probably kill off an alien, at long range, most speedily and effectively.

Cider was called " cidre " and " sithere " by fourteenth century writers ; and the word is said to be a corruption of the Greek *sikera*, used in the Septuagint to translate the Hebrew *shekar*, usually rendered " strong drink " in the Old Testament.

" The name of *Cider*," says one of these old writers, " if from *Sikera*, is but a general name for an inebriating or an intoxicating drink, and may argue their ignorance in those times of any other name than *Wine* for that liquor or juice in the Saxon or Norman language, either of those nations being unwilling (it's probable) to use a British name for so pleasing a drink, they not affecting the Britains, made use of few of their

words ; but since that, that wines have been
imported from foreign parts in great quantities,
the English have been forced to make use of the
old British name SEIDER, or *Cider*, for distinction
sake, although the name *vinum* may be as proper
for the juice of the apple as the grape, if it be
derived either from *Vi* or *Vincendo*, or *quasi
Divinum*, as one would have it. Also the vulgar
tradition of the scarcity of foreign wines in
England, viz. that Sack, which was then
imported for the most part but from Spain, was
sold in the apothecaries' shops as a cordial
medicine ; and the vast increase in vineyards in
France (Ale and Beer being usual drinks in Spain
and France in Pliny's time) is an argument sufficient
that the name of *Wine* might be attributed to
our British *Cider*, and of vineyards to the places
separated for the propagating the fruit that
yields it."

As a matter of fact the best cider in the
world is made in Normandy. And for what
purpose do the Normans make it ? To send
to the Champagne country to be sold to the
unsuspecting tourist as the sparkling wine of that
district. This is solid truth. Hundreds of
millions of gallons are made in Normandy with
the most scrupulous care, under the supervision
of experienced chemists, and the bulk is eventually sold as champagne. And not only champagne, but claret, white wines, and even honest,
manly, beautiful, unsophisticated, good old
Portuguese port, owe their being in some in-
stances to Normandy apples ; the rich colour of
the port being added by log-wood, beet-juice,

and the root of the rhatany. In fact, genuine port can be so closely imitated as to deceive many a good judge ; and it really seems wonderful that the British farmer does not go in for making port wine, with apples so plentiful and cheap, and beet, mangels, and elderberries so easy to cultivate. In fact, given the time, and the materials, I am convinced that I could produce an excellent '98 wine for laying down, for hospital purposes, public rejoicings, or *miladi's boudoir*.

Cider, like all other useful drinks, can be, and is, imitated ; and Bands of Hope and other well-meaning but misguided associations are chiefly responsible for this. What is known at Sunday - school treats and Salvation Army marriage-feasts as " non-alcoholic cider " has been found, on analysis, to be " a water solution of sugar and citric acid, flavoured with apple essence." It's the flavouring as does it.

" Harvest cider," as home-made for the " hands," is dreadful stuff, and absolutely unfit for human consumption. Apples which have fallen of themselves, or been blown off the trees, " windfalls," are left on the ground to rot, and be eaten of slugs and wasps ; and are then shovelled into the cider - mill, together with leaves, stalks, slugs, wasps, dirt of all sorts, spiders, ear-wigs, wire-worms, " Daddy Longlegs "-es, and—other things ; the whole being converted into a species of " hell-broth," which would have done credit to the best efforts of the witches in *Macbeth*, when properly mixed.

For a long time the Germans held aloof from

N

the manufacture of cider. The good Rhine wine, and the flowing and flatulent lager of their own country, were good enough for the Teutonic palate. But when it comes to a question of making money, with the risk reduced to a minimum, Germany seldom "gets left," as the Yankees say. Some of the inhabitants of the Fatherland discovered, about two decades ago, that there was *gelt* in cider, and since that time apples have been imported from France, by train-loads, for the purpose of being converted into cider. Germany now exports nearly twelve times as much of this fascinating beverage as does France ; and under whatever name it may figure in the bills—German Champagne, Military Port, Äpfel-wein, or Sparkling Hock—away goes the apple juice to all parts of the civilized world, including Damascus, Pekin, Khartoum, San Francisco, and Shaftesbury Avenue. In Frankfort-on-the-Maine alone there are more than fifty cider-factories, and the industry brings the town at least half a million sterling per annum.

"The fruits of the earth," says the ancient chronicler quoted above, "and especially of trees, were the first food ordained for man to eat."

And yet I had always understood that it was for eating an apple that our first parents were evicted from the garden. But to continue the quotation.

" And by eating of which (before flesh became his meat) he lived to a far greater age than since any have been observed to have lived. And of all the fruits our Northern parts produce, there's none more edible, nor more wholesome than *Apples ;*

which by the various preparations of the cook are become a part of our table entertainment almost throughout the year, and are esteem'd to be very temperate and nourishing.

" They relax the belly, which is a very good property in them ; but the sweet more than the sharp. They help concoction, eaten after meat, with a little bread : you may be confident that an apple eaten after supper "—paste this in your hats, ye revellers — " depresseth all offensive vapours that otherwise would offend the head, and hinder sleep. Apples rosted, scalded, or otherwise prepared, according to the skill of the operatour, are good in many hot diseases, against *Melancholy*, and the *Pleurisie*.

" But *Cider* is much to be preferr'd, it being the more pure and active part separated from the impure and feculent ; and without all, peradventure, is the most wholesome drink that is made in Europe for our ordinary use, as before is observed. For its specifick vertues, there is not any drink more effectual against the *Scurvy*. It is also prevalent against the *Stone*, and by its mundifying qualities is good against the diseases of the *Spleen*, and is esteem'd excellent against *Melancholy*."

Possibly the course of time has made us merrier than our forbears ; at all events " melancholy " is a disease for which no remedy is prescribed in the modern editions of the Pharmacopœia. What with musical farces, and Arthur Roberts, and the means to purchase a " livener " next morning, no citizen of London is justified in the possession of lowness of spirits.

Making cider is easy enough, but requires, like all other manufactures, care and a modicum of common sense. And here let me join issue with those who maintain that the inferiority of English cider is due to the antiquated methods employed in making it. In the first place I question the inferiority; and in the second, although it is a fact that there is very little difference between the methods of to-day and two hundred years ago, we are more careful, on the whole, in the selection of the material. Far more important than complicated machinery is the proper choice of apples. Grow these in a scientific way, and do not eat all the best for dessert. The cider apple should be neither green nor over-ripe—and certainly not rotten like those used occasionally for the harvesters—free from injury (and therefore not a " windfall ") and just full ripe. The selected fruit should be placed in a mill which breaks them up and pulps them; the pulp is then put under a press, and squeezed dry to the last drop. The liquid is then left to ferment, and this process should be very gradual, and be closely watched. Finally the cider is drawn off, the finest qualities being bottled, and they may be regarded as pure wine. At all events they are frequently sold " as sich."

It is claimed that cider, when pure and well made, is not merely an extremely wholesome drink, but a very helpful one to those who suffer from gout or rheumatism. It is asserted that cider will even cure these painful disorders, and that those who drink the juice of the apple are far less subject to aching joints and limbs than

other quaffers. It is the "malic acid" in the
liquor which is so inimical to these diseases ; and
as a cider-drinker of considerable experience, and
a sad sufferer, at times, from both diseases, I can
safely say that there is no "touch" of either in
the "natural" Norfolk cider made by Messrs.
Gaymer—a dry wine which is very palatable, and
is one of the best and the most wholesome of
beverages.

Cider at its strongest does not contain a large
percentage of alcohol, and its makers contend
that its qualities are more health-giving and far
less heady than those of any other liquor consumed in England. According to Mr. Radcliffe
Cooke, an enthusiast on the subject, the revival
in the cider industry dates from 1890, and there
is every hope that that industry will flourish more
and more, through the centuries. The recognized cider fruit may be divided into "bitter-
sweets"—such as the so-called Norman apples
and the Wildings—and the "red" fruits, such as
the nearly extinct "Red Streak." The best
cider is made from an admixture of the two sorts.
But the gout-fuge cider, we gather from another
writer, should be made from a *single* sort
of apple.

"There is no difficulty," writes Mr. Cooke,
"in expressing the apple juice ; but the fermentation process is not sufficiently studied, and it is
here that failure commonly occurs."

"As for the making of Perry and Cider,"
writes an authority of the seventeenth century,
"which are drinkes much used in the West parts,
and other countries well stored with fruit in this

kingdome ; you shall know that your perry is made of peares onely, and your cider of apples ; and for the manner of making thereof, it is done after one fashion, that is to say, after your Peares and Apples are well prickt from the stalkes, rottennesse, and all manner of other filthe, you shall put them in the presse mill which is made with a mil-stone running round in a circle, under which you shall crush your peares or apples, and then straining them through a bagge of haire cloth, tunne up the same (after it hath bene a little setled) into hogs-heads, barrels, and other close vessels.

" Now after you have prest all, you shall save that which is within the haire cloth bagge, and putting it into severall vessels, put a pretty quantity of water thereinto, and after it hath stood a day or two, and hath beene well stirred together, presse it over also againe, for this will make a small perry or cider, and must be spent first. Now of your best cider that which you make of your summer or sweete fruit you shall call summer or sweete cider or perry, and that you shall spend first also ; and that which you make of the winter and hard fruit, you shall call winter and sowre cider, or perry ; and that you may spend last, for it will indure the longest."

We don't boil much cider nowadays, but this was a custom in considerable favour with the ancients.

" In many places," says another writer, " they boyl their cider, adding thereto several spices, which makes it very pleasant, and abates the unsavoury smack it contracts by boyling, but withal gives it a high colour. This way is not to be commended, because the juice of the apple is either apt to extract some ill savour from the brass or copper, we being not acquainted with any other vessels to boyl it in, or the sediment of it is apt to burn by its adhering to the sides of the vessel, it being boyl'd in a naked fire.

"But if you are willing to boyl your cider, your vessel ought to be of *Latten*, which may be made large enough to boyl a good quantity, the *Tin* yielding no bad tincture to the liquor. . . . It many times happens that cider that hath been good, by ill-management or other accident becomes dead, flat, sowr, thick, muddy, or musty ; all which in some sort or other may be cured. You may cure deadness or flatness in cider by grinding a small parcel of apples, and putting them in at the bung-hole, and stopping it close, only sometimes trying it by opening the small vent that it force not the vessel ; but then you must draw it off in a few days, either into bottles or another vessel, lest the *Murc* corrupt the whole mass. Cider that is dead or flat will oftentimes revive again of itself, if close stopt, upon the revolution of the year and approaching summer."

Hippocras.

Here is an ancient recipe :—

Take of cardamoms, carpobalsamum, of each half an ounce, coriander-seeds prepared, nutmegs, ginger, of each two ounces, cloves two drachms ; bruise and infuse them two days in two gallons of the richest sweetest cider, often stirring it together, then add thereto of milk three pints, strain all through an hippocras bag, and sweeten it with a pound of sugar-candy.

D'you kna-ow—as the curate in *The Private Secretary* says—I am not taking any hippocras to-day.

" Wormwood imbib'd in cider," says another writer, " produceth the effect that it doth in wine." Evidently some nasty effect ; only con-ceive an admixture of absinthe and cider !

That the ancients loved mixtures—and sweet mixtures—is pretty evident from the writings of Pliny and others. Were a man to invite me to drink apple juice in the which had been bottled dried juniper-berries, I should probably hit that man in the eye, or send for a policeman. But two or three hundred years ago " juniper-cider " appears to have been a popular drink, although we read that " the taste thereof is somewhat strange, which by use will be much abated."

Ginger, cloves, cinnamon, currants, honey, rosemary, raspberries, blackberries, elderberries, and " clove-July-flowers," all used to be put into cider, by way of flavouring ; " but the best addi-tion," says the same writer, " that can be to it is that of the lees of *Malaga* Sack or Canary new and sweet, about a gallon to a hogshead ; this is a great improver and a purifier of cider."

Evidently in those days they had some crude sort of ideas on the subject of Cider Cup.

CHAPTER XVII

CORDIALS AND LIQUEURS

A chat about cherry brandy—Cherry gin—And cherry whisky—
Sloe gin — Highland cordial — What King Charles II.
swallowed—Poor Charles !—Ginger brandy—Orange-flower
brandy—Employment of carraway seeds—The school treat—
Use and abuse of aniseed—Do not drink quince whisky—
Try orange brandy instead—A hell-broth—Curaçoa—Cassis
—Chartreuse — The monks as benefactors — Some quaint
tavern " refreshers " — Kirschenwasser — Noyeau — Parfait
amour—Maraschino—A valuable ginger cordial.

LET us commence with that grand old British
eye-opener,

Cherry Brandy.

There are more ways than one of making
this. Here is an old recipe.

Take six dozen pounds of cherries, half red and
half black, and mash or squeeze them with your
hands to pieces, and put to them three gallons of
brandy, and let them stand steeping twenty-four
hours. Then put the mash'd cherries and liquor a
little at a time into a canvas bag, and press it as
long as any juice will run ; sweeten it to your taste,
and put it into a vessel fit for it, and let it stand a

month, and bottle it out ; put a lump of loaf-sugar into every bottle.

Another way, and a nicer ; the idea of squeezing cherries to pieces with the human hands savouring of barbarism—and fingers.

Take Black Geans or Black Morellos — but remember that the former are sweet, the latter acid and bitter, and there will be a great difference in the results. They must not be over-ripe. Take off the stalks, and if you choose prick them with a pin. Fill a bottle with them three-quarters, pour in brandy to the neck, and cork it up. It will be ready in a month.

It will be noticed that no mention of sugar is made in the above. The necessary quantity would naturally vary, according to the description of cherry employed.

Yet another—my way.

This can either be made from Black Gean cherries, or Morellos, but the latter are better for the purpose. Every pound of cherries will require one quarter of a pound of white sugar and one pint of the best brandy. The cherries, with the sugar well-mixed with them, should be placed in wide-mouthed bottles, filled up with brandy ; and if the fruit be previously pricked, the mixture will be ready in a month. But a better blend is procured if the cherries are untouched, and this principle holds good with all fruit treated in this way, and left corked for at least three months.

It should be borne in mind that these cordials are far better when home-made—provided always

the best materials be used.   The cherry brandy,
sloe gin, etc. etc., which is bought is not always
made with '65 cognac.   Remember how many
people have to make some sort of profit out of
what can be purchased over the counter.

One more way.

Put six pounds of black cherries, six pounds of
Morellos, and two pounds of strawberries in a cask.
Bruise them slightly with a stick, then add three
pounds of sugar, twelve cloves, half an ounce of
powdered cinnamon, and two grated nutmegs, with
a quarter of the kernels of the cherry-stones, and a
handful of mint and balm.   Pour over these six
quarts of brandy, and let the cask remain open for
ten days.   Then close it, and in two months it will
be fit for use.

Cherry Gin

can be made in the same way as any of the
above, merely substituting Old Tom for cognac.
And if you want to make it extra good, use
sugar-candy instead of the ordinary " best lump."

Cherry Whisky

was introduced to the public at the Brewers'
Exhibition in the Royal Agricultural Hall,
London, in 1898.   I have not tasted it, but
suppose that the method of making it is similar
to any of the above recipes, substituting Glenlivet.
But I fancy brandy or gin would always be
preferable ; for whisky does not blend well with
fruit.

Sloe Gin.

The difference between this cordial as made
at home, and allowed to mature gradually, and
the stuff retailed in taverns, is marked. 'Tis a
"refresher" which has only become popular
within the last few years; and consequently
within a radius of twenty miles from London,
the sloe-bushes are stripped of their fruit, before
it is fit to pick, by the poorer classes, who can
obtain sixpence per pound—or something like
that price—for sloes in the market. But the sloe
should not be picked for this purpose until it has
experienced at least one night's frost.

Allow one pound of sugar to one pound of sloes.
Half fill an ordinary quart bottle with sugared sloes,
and fill up with gin. If the sloes have been
previously pricked, the liqueur will be fit for use in
a couple of months; but 'tis better *not* to prick
them, but let the gin do its own work of extraction.
In that case the bottle should not be uncorked
within twelve months.

A great deal of the alleged sloe gin sold is
light in colour, and has evidently been hurried in
its preparation. A great deal more is quite
innocent of sloe juice, and is merely inferior gin,
diluted and coloured. The orthodox sloe gin
should bear the hue of "fruity" port wine. See
that you get it.

Highland Cordial.

Here is another recipe into which the wine
of bonnie Scotland enters. At one time the

cordial was popular with the Scots, who now, however, prefer their whisky unadorned.

Steep in one bottle of old Scotch whisky one pint of white currants, stripped of their stalks, the thin rind of a lemon, and one teaspoonful of essence of ginger. Let the mixture stand for forty-eight hours, and then strain through a hair sieve. Add one pound of loaf-sugar, which will take at least a day to thoroughly dissolve. Then bottle off and cork well. It will be ready for use in three months, but will keep longer.

A cordial which is but seldom asked for nowadays was known in the seventeenth century as

King Charles II.'s Surfeit-Water.

Take a gallon of the best aqua-vitæ, and a quart of brandy, and a quart of anniseed-water, a pint of poppy-water, and a pint of damask-rose-water ; put these in a large glass jar, and put to it a pound of fine powdered sugar, a pound and a half of raisins stoned, a quarter of a pound of dates stoned and sliced, one ounce of cinnamon bruised, cloves one ounce, four nutmegs bruised, one stick of licorice scraped and sliced ; let all these stand nine days close covered, stirring three or four times a day ; then add to it three pounds of fresh poppies, or three handfuls of dried poppies, a sprig of angelica, two or three of balm ; so let it stand a week longer, then strain it out and bottle it.

And then notify the undertaker, I should think. The Merry Monarch had his faults, but, surfeit or no surfeit, it is hard to believe that a king could bring himself to lap such a

" hell-broth " as the above.   Pah ! Let us take the taste out with

Ginger Brandy.

Bruise slightly two pounds of black currants, and mix them with one ounce and a half of ground ginger.   Pour over them one bottle and a half of best old brandy, and let the mixture stand for two days.   Strain off the liquid, and add one pound of loaf-sugar which has been boiled to a syrup in a little water.   Bottle and cork closely.

Orange-flower Brandy.

There is not much of this in the market, or the store-cupboard.

Take a gallon of best brandy, and mix with it a pound of orange-flowers which have been boiled. Save the water, sweeten it, and bottle off the mixture.

Carraway Brandy.

Steep an ounce of carraway seeds and six ounces of loaf-sugar in a quart of brandy.   Let this stand nine days, then strain and bottle.

And the author of the above adds : " 'Tis a good cordial."   Three hundred years ago carraways invariably figured at the dessert-table in England.   The seeds now appear either in cakes for school-treats, sugar-plums, or the favourite liqueur known as

Kümmel.

This is principally made in Russia, and is an excellent stomachic.   Own brother to the carraway seed is the anise seed, which appears in a liqueur, made chiefly at Bordeaux, and called

Anisette.

Personally, I prefer Kümmel, and the other is more of a drug than an enlivening potion. Cough remedies for the most part contain anise seed, which is also largely used at a "drag" hunt, hounds being especially keen on the scent.

Apricot Brandy.

This is not often met with away from its home in the United States.

To every pound of fruit (which should not be quite ripe) add one pound of loaf-sugar. Put the apricots into a preserving-pan, with sufficient water to cover them. Let them boil up, and then simmer gently until tender. Remove the skins. Clarify and boil the sugar, then pour it over the fruit, and let it remain twenty-four hours. Then put the apricots into wide-mouthed bottles, and fill them up with syrup and brandy, half and half. Cork tightly, and seal the tops of the corks.

This apricot brandy should be prepared in the month of July, and kept at least twelve months before using.

Quince Whisky.

I once superintended the brew of a decoction of quinces and Scotch whisky. The quinces were treated exactly as the apricots are in the above recipe, and we kept the stuff bottled up for a year. I don't think I ever tasted anything nastier.

Orange Brandy

should be made in the month of March, and, well-made, is the best of all cordials, being especially valuable on a cold morning just before proceeding with the hounds to draw Newton Wood.

Take the thin rinds of six Seville oranges, and put them into a stone jar, with half a pint of the strained juice and half a gallon of good old brandy. Let it remain three days, then add one pound and a quarter of loaf-sugar—broken, not pounded—and stir till the sugar is dissolved. Let the liquor stand a day, strain it through paper until quite clear, pour into bottles, and cork tightly. The longer it is kept the better.

The ancients apparently interpreted the word "cordial" in a different way to our later way; and their cordials were chiefly used in the sick-room.

The Saffron Cordial,

for instance, was chiefly employed to cure fainting fits, the ague, and the smallpox. I think I should have preferred all three complaints at once.

Fill a large still with marigold flowers, and strew on it an ounce of ground nutmeg; beat them grosly, and take an ounce of the best English saffron, pull it, and mix with the flowers; then take three pints of muscadine or tent, or Malaga sack, and with a sprig of rosemary dash it on the flowers; then distil it off with a slow fire, and let it drop on

white sugar-candy; draw it off till it begins to be
sowre, save a pint of the first running to mix with
other waters on an extraordinary occasion; mix the
rest together to drink by itself. Take five or six
spoonfuls at a time.

As Hamlet observes, on a memorable occasion :
" Oh, horrible, horrible, most horrible ! "

Curaçoa

is not only the best known of all liqueurs, but
the most wholesome.   It will blend equally well
with brandy and whisky.   The best, in fact
the original brand, is made in Amsterdam, with
the peel of a very rare orange which grows in
the island of Curaçoa, and falls from the tree
before it is ripe.   The peel of this is dried, and
is known in the trade as the Curaçoa of Holland,
to distinguish it from other Curaçoas which have
not the same property, although they are often
sold in place of it.   The Dutch distillers naturally
keep their process a secret, but the French
imitators declare that the Dutch secret is merely
as follows : that five kilogrammes of dried peel
of the Curaçoa of Holland and the zests of eighty
fresh oranges are submitted to the action of sixty
litres of alcohol (85 degrees, French measure-
ment), and that, save in the colour, there is
no real difference between white Curaçoas and
brown.   At all events either is very useful in a
cocktail, or swizzle ; and there are many restorative compounds, or " tonics " as they are called,
into which the liqueur enters.

o

Cassis,

owing to the ridiculously-high duty imposed
upon its importation, is comparatively unknown
in England, although it can be obtained at every
little roadside *cabaret* in France, cheap enough.
The cassis of Dijon has a great reputation as a
cooling drink.   There is an infinitesimal portion
of alcohol in it, and it can, I should say, be easily
made at home by anybody who possesses some
nice ripe black-currants.   Still the nearest the
ordinary English householder gets to cassis is in
the manufacture of so-called "black-currant
tea"; and you only get that when you have a
sore throat.

Chartreuse.

One of the most severe sects of monks manufacture a liqueur which is the highest prized and
priced of all, for the benefit of Sybarites who
deny themselves no luxury in life.   St. Bruno
the founder of this order chose for his monastery
the most desolate and barren spot he could find
in the mountains of Dauphiné, and forbade his
followers to eat the flesh of bird or beast ; the
fruit of the vine and strong waters being likewise
defended.   But one of them discovered, nevertheless, that a most seductive liquid could be
distilled from plants, chief amongst them being
Angelica Archangelica—a plant which it is probable did not receive its holy name until trial had
been made of the distillation.   The Carthusian
monks have the sole right of selling this liqueur
—a right which brings them in a very substan-

tial revenue ; for Chartreuse is esteemed—in France, at all events—above all *chasses*. The yellow kind is the best, and the white mildest of the three, of which the green is fiery. Personally, I prefer curaçoa, or, better still, cognac '65.

The name of the " little refreshers " consumed at tavern-bars in large cities is legion. I have heard the following compounds called for, at different times : sherry-and-bitters—there being at least half a dozen sorts of bitters—gin-and-ditto, whisky-and-ditto ; vermouth (Italian or French), vermouth-and-sloe-gin, gin-and-sherry, gin-and-orange-gin, sloe-gin, gin-and-sloe-gin (commonly called " slow-and-quick "), curaçoa-and-brandy, whisky alone, brandy alone, gin alone. And in the Borough there is a dreadful mixture known by the appropriate name of

Twist.

" This," says an esteemed correspondent, " is a favourite liqueur of the porters in the hop-warehouses. You go into the ' Red Cross,' for instance, and ask for a ' 'alf-quartern o' Twist in a three-out glass,' and you will find that it consists of equal parts of rum and gin, and is a powerful pick-me-up after a wet night."

I should question the " pick-me-up " part of this story ; therefore shall not schedule " Twist " in my list of Restoratives, in the next chapter.

Kirschenwasser.

This is a wholesome and reviving liqueur made from the cherries which grow in the Black Forest. It is not as potent as maraschino, which is also made from cherries, in another place. But the Black Forest cherry-water requires a little treatment to render it palatable.

Put a little in a saucer ; take a lump of sugar, set fire to it, and replace it in the saucer, so that the rest of the liquid may be set ablaze. When the flame is burnt out and the sugar melted, the liqueur is fit to drink.

Noyeau

is made from white brandy and apricot-kernels, and is the sweetest, as well as the most pernicious of all liqueurs. I do not know how many glasses it would take to kill an ordinary man, but most people know that noyeau contains hydrocyanic acid of which none but those tired of the world would care to drink too much.

Parfait Amour

"What's in a name ? " This is simply bad orange-bitters, and there is neither love nor perfection in it. But they say that in dear old England, in the olden time, before oranges could be bought at three-halfpence per dozen, it was customary for a lover, on New Year's Day, to present his sweetheart with an orange stuck all over with cloves, as an emblem of Perfect Love. The sweetheart of to-day prefers a bangle, or a bicycle.

One more liqueur,

Maraschino.

This is a bitter-sweet liqueur made at Zara from the kernel of the Marasca cherry, or gean

of Dalmatia.   The word implies bitterness, yet
the liquid is sweet enough to catch flies.   " It is
a curious fact," says a modern writer, " in natural
history that the fair sex prefer a sweet liqueur to
the finest wine ; and they have such a tendency
to maraschino that Mr. Hayward has proposed
that whereas the toast most honoured among
men is Wine and Women, they should adopt as
their own return toast—Men and Maraschino."

The French make different imitations of the
true liqueur, one of them from peach-stones,
which they call " Marasquin de pêches."   And
in the true Maraschino of Zara there be a few
peach-stones mixed with those of the geans.
These are small and quite black, and are fermented first with honey, then with the leaves
and kernels of the fruit, and are last of all distilled
and sweetened with sugar.

One more cordial, to finish the chapter.   The
recipe was given in the *Lady's Pictorial*, by Mrs.
C. E. Humphry, the delightful and ever-welcome
" Madge " of *Truth*.   I can vouch for the
efficacy of the potion.

Ginger Cordial.

Two quarts of Scotch whisky, three lemons sliced,
one ounce of ground ginger, half an ounce of carraway seeds, three pounds of lump-sugar, one ounce of
bitter almonds, three ounces of sweet almonds, one
pound of raisins.   Put all into a crock, and stir every
day for three weeks.   Then strain through three
folds of blotting-paper, or one fold of filtering-paper,
and bottle.

CHAPTER XVIII

THE AFTERMATH OF REVELRY

Revelry means remorse—And "Katzenjammer"—And other things—Why will ye do it?—The devil in solution—Alcoholism a disease — An accountant on wires — A jumpy journalist—A lot of jolly dogs—What is "Langdebeefe"? —To cure spleen or vapours—Directly opposite effects of alcohol—The best pick-me-up in the world—An anchovy toast—Baltimore egg nogg—Orange quinine—About brandy and soda-water—A Scorcher — Brazil relish — St. Mark's pick-me-up — A champion bitters — A devilled biscuit— Restorative sandwiches—Fresh air and exercise best of all— Stick to your nerve!

THIS is a world of compensations. Therefore it is of no use shutting our eyes to the fact that for every minute of injudicious, over-estimated revelry, of devotion to the rosy god, passed at night in the best of society, with boon companions, we are liable to an hour's disturbance, worry, agony of mind, headache, remorse of conscience, "jim-jams," "Katzenjammer" (the equivalent for "hot coppers")—call it what you will, next day. Some suffer for over-indulgence more than others. There be so-called "seasoned casks" who claim that no amount of debauchery can affect them for the worse, as long as the liquor be good, and not swallowed too quickly. But, although these may "come up smiling" next day, on making their first public appearance, the collapse, the downfall is only postponed. Without being able to explain these things medically, it is certain that Alcohol—which is, as previously explained, the Devil in Solution— will destroy in the end, if you abuse her, although her methods of destruction may differ, according to the capacity, or constitution, of her victims.

And let not the over-estimator expect any sympathy from the world, or any part of it, whilst he is experiencing the "remorse of conscience" stage. Katzenjammer patients are sternly and forcibly refused admission to any public hospitals, even if *in extremis;* for mercy, charity, and the medical faculty have refused hitherto to recognize the fact that alcoholism is a disease. And he who is "jumpy" and nervous of a morning has just as much chance of obtaining condolence from friends or relatives as has the casual sufferer from gout. Both disorders are, in fact, excellent provocatives of badinage and laughter.

I remember hearing of an accountant in Cape Town, a hardened and determined "night bird," a frequenter of hostelries, a boon companion—in short, a sot. He was called as a witness in an intricate case in the High Court, one morning, whilst suffering terribly from nerves. It was heart-rending to watch his agony. His features twitched, his eyes rolled, and his hands shook as though afflicted with palsy on the higher scale. The ledgers which

were occasionally handed up to him by the usher,
for reference, slipped from his grasp, and docu-
mentary testimony flew all over the counsels'
wigs. At length the notice of the judge was
attracted to the state of things.

"What is the matter with that witness?"
asked his lordship. "Is he trifling with the
court?"

"M'lord," said counsel for the plaintiff, "I
am instructed that the witness is what may be
called a free-liver, and that it is often necessary
for him to swallow a dram in the morning, before
proceeding to business. I am also instructed
that the witness overslept himself this morning,
and had no time to procure the necessary dose,
before appearing as a witness before your lordship."

"Tut, tut!" exclaimed the judge. "This
is wasting the time of the court. Let him be
removed at once to the waiting-room and dosed
with old brandy."

He was a practical judge ; and in five minutes'
time that accountant had pulled himself together.

And an even more painful case than the
above is within my memory. A certain news-
paper-proprietor was in the habit of paying the
weekly wages of his staff himself, each member
having to sign a receipt for the reward of merit.
The fashion - editor — a hardened libertine —
turned up one Saturday, before his chief,
absolutely incapable of signing his name, or any
part of it. His gait was all right, as was his
speech ; but the pen slipped through his fingers
as though it had been a well-oiled icicle. The

chief called the next case, the while some of us
poured over-proof rum down the throat of the
fashion - editor at an adjacent hostelry. He
subsequently trousered his salary, and signed the
receipt, satisfactorily, after pleading that he was
suffering that morning from " shock."

The chief looked somewhat incredulous.

" Is he an inebriate ? " he asked, as soon as
the invalid had left the office.

" Oh ! dear no, sir," replied the acrostic-
editor, " he's almost a teetotaller."

And the incident was finished.

But what is really the best thing to be done
under such sad circumstances ?   Should the
invalid resort to the old remedy, and take at
once that " hair of the dog " who bit him overnight ?   Not invariably.   For instance, should
British port, or brandy of the desiccated-window-
sill (*vide* a former chapter) have been the *causa
teterrima* of the trouble, nobody, however shaky,
would revert to such remedies, the first thing
after waking.   And frequently it is difficult for
the waker to remember *which* dog it was that
assaulted him.   I once visited a young friend in
his chambers, at the hour of noon, and found
him with a sad countenance, seated in an easy-
chair faced by a perfect army of assorted bottles.
I was about to administer a mild reproof, but he
stopped me.

' It's all right, dear old chappie, I've been
taking a hair of the dog—*you* know.   But I met
such a lot of dogs, jolly dogs too, last night,
that I'm hanged if I can remember which of 'em
bit me ! "

The ancients cooled their coppers, for the most part, with ale, either small or large. And I am led to the belief that cider, or some preparation of apples, was also used as a pick-me-up, if " melancholy vapours "—a complaint for which Gervase Markham specially recommended cider as a specific—meant the same thing as alcoholic remorse.   Search as I may I can find no recipe, no prescription, in old books for " hot coppers."   Can it be that the ancients, who as previously pointed out, were *not* teetotallers, deceived themselves in protesting before men that they had no sin ?

Here is an old recipe headed :

" *Against Drunkennesse.*

" If you would not be drunke, take the powder of *Betany* and *Coleworts* mix't together ; and eat it every morning fasting, as much as will lie on a sixpence, and it will preserve a man from drunkennesse."

But this is an alleged preventive of the act, and not a chaser of sorrow from the brow of the unwise partaker.

" To quicken a man's wits," writes the same Mr. Markham, " spirit and memory, let him take Langdebeefe "—can this mean *langue de bœuf?*—" which is gathered in June or July, and beating it in a cleane mortar ; Let him drinke the juyce thereof with warme water, and he shall finde the benefit."

Probably the most useful part of this prescription was the warm water ; still it can hardly be regarded as a restorative.

Other recipes are before me, for " drawing
out bones broken in the head," and " for the
falling of the mould of the head " ; but these,
apparently, have no concern with the question
at issue.   But to continue the search—*eureka!*

" *To Cure Spleen or Vapours.*

Take an ounce of the filings of steel, two
drachms of gentian sliced, half an ounce of
carduns seeds bruised, half a handful of centaury
tops ; infuse all these in a quart of white wine
four days, and drink four spoonfuls of the clear
every morning, fasting two hours after it, and
walking about."

This I take to be a *bona fide* pick-me-up of
two hundred years ago ; and if " carduns" be the
old spelling of " cardamom " 'tis very much the
same mixture that the chemist will place in the
trembling hand of the over-estimator, enquiring
at the same time, " Would you like a lozenge
after it, sir ? "   And the omission of sal volatile
or chloric ether in the prescription leads to the
belief that those drugs were joys unknown to
the reveller of the seventeenth century.

The most aggravating part about the aftermath of revelry is that it takes, just as it likes,
directly opposite forms.   Two sinners may jump
the same stiff course—by this sporting metaphor
is meant imbibe the same amount and description
of alcohol—after dinner, and, whilst A may wake
with a double-breasted headache, a taste of sewage
in the mouth, and a tongue as foul and furry as
a stoat's back, B will commence the day with a

dreadful sinking at the base of the stomach, pal-
pitation of the heart, and a desire to eat anything solid within reach.   A prays faintly for
burnt brandy, or death, and could not swallow
even a devilled biscuit, were you to promise to
make him a director of a gold-mine for performing
that feat ; whilst B is " dead off " brandy, but is
capable of washing down ham and eggs and
chops unlimited, with a gallon or two of coffee.
Any medical man will doubtless give a reason
for this discrepancy, which is quite beyond my
powers of elucidation.

The Best Pick-me-up

known to the writer is " the Boy, the whole
Boy, and nothing but the Boy." 'Tis an expensive restorative, no doubt ; but, just as you cannot make an omelette without breaking eggs,
so are most of our pleasant vices more or less
costly in the long-run.   Champagne, *i.e.* genuine
champagne, is about the most valuable restorative
known to science, and has—I believe, though
this is not within my own experience—saved the
lives of sufferers from the " black death," cholera.
Whether blended with beaten eggs, bitters, or
brandy, or in his pure natural beauty, there is,
believe me, no such effectual sorrow - chaser as
" The Boy."

Anchovy Toast.

The next best restorer of the faculties is a
quasi-solid ; and the recipe for its concoction has
already been given in *Cakes and Ale.* As, how-

ever, a portion of the public may be fated to enjoy the ale without the cakes, here it is again.

First and foremost, bear in mind that this appetizer must not be made in the kitchen. It comes under the heading of " parlour cookery," and can even be manufactured in the bedroom of the sufferer.

A hot-water plate is necessary for the operator, or, better still, a slop-basin filled with water as near the boiling point as possible, with a plate placed atop. Melt on this plate a piece of butter about the size of a walnut, and when the butter is oiled stir therein with a fork the beaten yolk of one egg. Keep on the stir, and add, gradually, a dessert spoonful of essence of anchovies. Add cayenne, according to your disposition, or indisposition, and then you will be ready for a nice strip or two of delicately-browned toast, brought up hot from the kitchen fire. Soak the toast in the mixture, and eat as much as you can.

Above is the estimate for *one* invalid. It is essentially a pick-me-up for a bachelor—benedicts never require these things—and if, whilst in barracks, or chambers, Jack, Tom, and Harry should call, the proportions of the ingredients must, of course, be increased. A glass or two of the Boy will be found to go down excellent well with this toast, the secret of which I learnt long years ago, in British India. It is *not* a dish for the dinner-table.

A

Baltimore Egg Nogg

reads like a " large order." It is said by its

author to be "an excellent drink for debilitated people, and a nourishing diet for consumptives." And he would be a Good Samaritan, who would wait outside the big gates of Holloway Castle, on a Monday morning, in order to administer the nogg, in full doses, to the starved captives on their release. It would also, I should imagine, make an excellent hospital drink, for a score or so of patients.

Beat the yolks of sixteen eggs and twelve table-spoonfuls of pulverized loaf-sugar to the consistency of cream ; stir into this two-thirds of a grated nut-meg, and then pour in half a pint of good old brandy, or Jamaica rum—or both *n.q.*—and three wine-glasses of Madeira. Have ready the whites of the sixteen eggs, whipped to a stiff froth, and beat them well into the above mixture, and then stir in six pints of new milk, as fresh as possible from the cow.

One of the best restoratives is that which is frequently given by the trainer of an athlete, or boxer, should his charge feel the effects of over-work. It consists of the heart of a good loin chop, free from fat, and neither underdone nor overdone, on a very hot plate, with a glass of port wine poured over the meat. Another familiar strengthener is prepared in the following way :—

Put a tablespoonful of old brandy into half a pint of good beef-tea. And by beef-tea I mean the juices of the meat extracted at home, and not by the employées of advertising firms. "Breakfast deli-cacies" and tinned preparations are only for the unwary. This may be taken either hot or cold.

Orange Quinine

is an excellent tonic.

To a pint bottle of orange wine add ten grains of sulphate of quinine, cork well, and let it stand for a few days.   Take a wine-glassful at a time, either with or without a dash of soda-water.

Brandy-and-Soda,

already alluded to in an earlier chapter, will get no recommendation from me, as a restorative. If quite certain of your soda-water, and of your brandy, a tumblerful on occasion will do no harm ; but do not be in too great a hurry to order this, after meeting an old friend, in a strange district.   Like Wotsisname's pills, the more brandy-and-sodas you take, the more you will want ; and the tendency of soda-water is distinctly lowering.   As for bad soda-water— well, it will kill almost as rapidly as will bad brandy.

A favourite restorative of the working man, who has been propounding abstruse political problems in the tap-room all night, is a red-herring, eaten raw, with the aid of his clasp-knife.   This he will wash down with some sort of ale, or with a mixture of gin-and-peppermint, according to the state of his feelings.   That old, heroic soberer the Pump, is not much used for that purpose, nowadays.

A Scorcher

is a rarely-employed pick-me-up.   It consists of

the juice of half a lemon squeezed into a large wine-glass, a liqueur-glass of old brandy being added, and a dash of cayenne.

I have already alluded in another chapter to a Prairie Oyster. A Worcester Oyster is made in the same way, with the substitution of Worcester sauce for vinegar.

Brazil Relish.

This reads far more like an emetic than a "livener"; but I am assured by one who has been in Brazil—"where the nuts come from"— and in the regions which border on the river Plate, that 'tis used in those parts as a stimulant, and is in high favour for that purpose.

Into a wine-glass half full of curaçoa pop the unbroken yolk of a bantam's egg, and fill the glass up with maraschino. I think I should prefer the "Twist" of the workers in the Borough hop-market.

St. Mark's Pick-me-up,

a Venetian recipe. The original St. Mark never wanted it.

Ten drops of Angostura bitters in a wine-glass, filled up with orange-bitters. One wine-glassful of old brandy, one ditto cold water, one liqueur-glassful of curaçoa, and the juice of half a lemon. This, I should say, ought to be mixed with a swizzle-stick.

Here follows a very old, and a very excellent, recipe for

Bitters

for mixing purposes.

One ounce of Seville orange-peel, half an ounce of gentian-root, a quarter of an ounce of cardamoms. Husk the cardamoms, and crush them with the gentian-root. Put them in a wide-mouthed bottle, and cover with brandy or whisky. Let the mixture remain for twelve days, then strain, and bottle off for use, after adding one ounce of lavender drops.

A hot-pickle sandwich may be made with two thin, crisp slices of toast, with chopped West-Indian pickles in between. There are also many excellent sandwiches made for restorative purposes, by the nymphs who enliven the various Bodegas by their abilities and pretty prattle. And of those sandwiches commend me to the one labelled " Rajah."

To make a

Devilled Biscuit

take a plain cheese-biscuit, heat it, but do not scorch it, in the oven. Then spread over it a paste composed of finely-powdered lobster worked up with butter, made mustard, ground ginger, cayenne, salt, Chili vinegar, and (if you can stand it) a little curry powder. Reheat the biscuit for a short time, and then deal with it.

But, after all, fresh air and exercise are the best of all restoratives ; and most of the above recipes are adduced in the interest of the jaded Londoner, or the dweller in cities, to whom a ride, or a walk, save on Sundays and Bank holidays,

P

is a rarity. Get on your hack and gallop a
dozen miles to covert. By the time you have
mounted your first hunter, you will have forgotten all about the dog which may have bitten
you on the previous night, and will also have
forgotten a stern resolution made, whilst
shying at your breakfast, never again to put
whisky, however old, atop of claret. And
by the time you have jumped three ox-fences,
and a great yawning drain big enough and deep
enough to bury the whole field, you will have
recovered every bit of that " nerve " about which
you had just a suspicion of a doubt, just before
mounting your hack. God grant that nerve
may be with you always !

CHAPTER XIX

THE DRINKS OF DICKENS

ALTHOUGH it is the fashion of the day to be-
little, if not sneer at, the works of " Boz," he has
still sufficient admirers to justify a chapter on
what is, I hope, a congenial subject to my
readers. The characters may be unduly elabor-
ated, and the incidents too much spun-out for
these slap-dash, go-ahead times ; but it is to the
simple, homely, hospitality so often referred to
in the novels of Charles Dickens that most of
them owed that popularity which may, or may

not, be on the wane.   The close student of these
novels will discover that all which is good, and
honest, and upright, and charitable is honoured
in their pages, whilst meanness, deceit, hypocrisy,
and cant are lashed with no uncertain hand.
"The greatest of all gifts is Charity," is the
lesson taught by Charles Dickens, who shewed
at the same time that it is quite possible to enjoy
the good things of life without making a beast
of oneself.   And he it was who clothed Christmas in that warm, sumptuous robe of joviality and
hospitality which makes all who keep that festival
in the proper spirit forget for the time that a
quarter's rent falls due on the same day.

Dickens's drunkards are few and far between
—and in this category I do not include such as
Sydney Carton, the members of the Pickwick
Club, and David Copperfield, on the occasion
of his first dinner-party.   Nobody has a right to
call the man who makes merry with his friends,
now and then, a sot ; and a careful study of
Dickens shows that the real inebriates, the
"habituals" described in his works, had all more
or less rascality in their composition—not even
excepting Dick Swiveller, who, however, became
a reformed character towards the close of the
book.

As for the drinks themselves, it is especially
worthy of note that there is no mention whatever
made of whisky in these works ; a fact which
justifies everything which I have written in a
former chapter as to the neglect with which this
undoubtedly estimable and wholesome fortifier
was treated by society, until within the last few

decades. A brandy-and-soda was an unknown fact during the Dickens period ; simply because, although there was plenty of brandy, the true virtues of soda-water had not been discovered. Moreover, nobody was known to call for a gin-and-bitters, or a sherry-and-angostura ; whilst cocktails and cobblers are mentioned only in the American chapters of *Martin Chuzzlewit*. Ales and beers were known by various fantastic names during the first half of the present century, when men knew not " four-'alf " nor " bitter-six " ; thus we have little David Copperfield gravely asking for a glass of the " Genuine Stunning," whilst Mrs. Gamp was unable to fulfil her arduous duties satisfactorily without a generous allowance of " the Brighton old Tipper."

But to the books themselves. And commencing with *David Copperfield*—who is provided with the heart, feelings, and understanding of the great novelist himself — I make my first pause at the waiter at the Yarmouth hotel. I don't like that waiter, either as a man or a waiter ; and his portrait by " Phiz " suggests a Cheap Jack at a fair, or a barber, rather than a coffee - room attendant. As a boy, I always looked up to a waiter as a benefactor—a species of Santa Claus, and not as a marauding varlet who would probably despoil me of my lawful share of the banquet and then lie about the incident to the landlady. And when this rascal pleads that he " lives on broken wittles, and sleeps on the coals," I lose patience with him. A waiter who could rob a poor boy of his beer would not need to sleep on the coals. He might have been a tax-gatherer, or a bailiff.

Mr. Creakle, the schoolmaster, appears to have been a bit of an imbiber, whilst the boys themselves partook, *sub rosa*, of cowslip wine, occasionally fortified by Steerforth with orange juice, ginger, or a peppermint drop ; and it was probably due to this decoction, rather than to " Crab," that poor Traddles became ill in the night—his sufferings being unduly prolonged by black draughts and blue pills, not to mention six chapters of Greek Testament and a special-extra caning. Poor little David partook or assorted drinks during his boyhood, including the aforesaid " Genuine Stunning," and occasional wine-glasses of punch whilst lodging with the Micawber family ; and, his good aunt once found, " her first proceeding was to unlock a tall press, bring out several bottles, and pour some of the contents of each into my mouth. I think they must have been taken out at random, for I am sure I tasted aniseed water, anchovy sauce, and salad dressing."

" My aunt " partook of hot white wine and water, with strips of toast soaked therein, by way of a night-cap ; and whenever Micawber turns up, we may be sure that the ingredients for a bowl of punch (presumably rum punch) are not far off. Not much drinking was done in the Peggotty family, but Mrs. Crupp, David's landlady, seems to have had the proverbial passion of her race for brandy ; and, naturally enough, the " handy young man " hired to wait, on the occasion of the dinner to Steerforth, got more

than his fair share of the wines.   Mr. Wickfield
—silly old dotard to be deceived by such a
shallow, transparent ruffian as Uriah Heep—
drank assorted wines to drown his cares ; whilst
one of the servants engaged by Dora, during
her brief experience of matrimonial joys, used
to chalk up an account, in her mistress' name,
at the public house, the items appearing as
"half-quartern gin and cloves (Mrs. C.) ; " "glass
rum and peppermint (Mrs. C.) "—the parenthesis
always referring to Dora, who was supposed to
have consumed the whole of these refreshments.

There is a fair amount of assorted drinking in
Martin Chuzzlewit.   Revelry at Pecksniff Hall
took, we learn, the form of red and white currant
wine, of acid characteristics, the remains of the
two bottles being subsequently blended, for the
special malefit of Tom Pinch and young Martin.
But the artful Pecksniff himself did not stir
without the brandy bottle when going on a
journey, and the family seem to have done themselves particularly well at "Todgers's."   Whenever I feel more than ordinarily depressed in
spirits, I overhaul my *Martin Chuzzlewit* and
read, once again, the report of the dinner at
Todgers's, which led to Mr. Pecksniff's fall into
the fireplace.   John Westlock—about the most
admirable young man in all Dickens's novels—
did not forget to do his friends well at Salisbury.
"As to wines," we are told, "the man who can
dream such iced champagne, such claret, port, or
sherry, had better go to bed and stop there."

The blackmailing of the captain of the *Screw*
by the proprietor of the *New York Rowdy Journal*

took the form of champagne ; and the merits of
a sherry cobbler are fully recognized by Martin,
who subsequently, however, fared badly in the
way of wines and spirits whilst in the States.
Eden, that alleged "prosperous city," appears to
have possessed neither pawn-shop, place of
worship, nor drinking-bar ; and the comparative
delights of the "Dragon" on the return of Mark
and Martin to Wiltshire are made delightfully
apparent.   As for the bad characters, Chevy
Slyme loafed in a chronic state of eleemosynary
drink, until he joined the police force, whilst
Montague Tigg fared sumptuously on the best
of liquor—including old Maderia—until knocked
on the head by the villain Jonas, who also appears
to have been a bit of a soaker, when he could
get his drink for nothing.

Mrs. Gamp's wants were few and simple, but
she insisted upon a regular supply, and got it.
Leaving solid sustenance out, she stipulated for
"a pint of mild porter at lunch, a pint at dinner,
half a pint as a species of stay or holdfast between
dinner and tea, and a pint of the celebrated
staggering ale, or Real Old Brighton Tipper, at
supper ; besides the bottle on the chimney-piece,
and such casual invitations to refresh herself with
wine as the good breeding of her employers
might prompt them to offer."   And she never
exceeded the allowance of a shillingsworth of
gin-and-water warm when she rang the bell a
second time after supper.   She must have cost
as much to keep as a steam-yacht.   The contents
of Mrs. G.'s teapot, on the occasion of her
historic quarrel with Betsy Prig, are alluded to,

vaguely, by the novelist as "spirits," and were, I shall ever maintain, gin, and *not* rum, as stated by other reviewers. The idea of putting rum on the top of "Newcastle salmon, intensely pickled," and such a monstrous (to a *connoisseur* in these things) salad as that furnished by Mrs. Prig, is barbaric.

After an experience of the modern roadside inn, or of the "reserved lounges" of the alcohol-palaces of to-day, what can be more delightful reading than the description of the interior of the "Maypole," in *Barnaby Rudge?*

"The very snuggest, cosiest, and completest bar that ever the wit of man devised. Such amazing bottles in old oaken pigeon-holes ; such gleaming tankards hanging from pegs at about the same inclination as thirsty men would hold them to their lips ; such sturdy little Dutch kegs ranged in rows on shelves ; so many lemons hanging in separate nets, suggestive, with goodly loaves of sugar stowed away hard by, of punch, idealized beyond all mortal knowledge, etc. etc."

Hardly an ideal landlord of the past, though, was old John Willet. A far better stamp of host was Gabriel Varden, the locksmith, who took deep draughts of sparkling home-brewed ale, from a goodly jug of well-browned clay, for breakfast, and who was one of the "Maypole's" best customers. Mr. Chester—whose interview with his son will remind the student of Monsieur le Marquis's interview with his nephew, in *A Tale of Two Cities*—was a judge of wine, though not given to over-indulgence in the bowl, like his bastard, Maypole Hugh ; and Lord George

Gordon's favourite brew appears to have been hot mulled wine. As for the rest of the rioters, they drank, after the manner of rioters, anything they could get.

The first mention of wine in *A Tale of Two Cities* is the fall and breakage, *pro bono publico*, of a large cask of inferior claret in the district of St. Antoine—emblematic of the blood to be spilt in Paris later on—which called forth the delightful, philosophic remark of Defarge, the master of the wine-shop to which the cask had been consigned: "It is not my affair. The people from the market did it. Let them bring another." But the chief imbibers in the book are Sydney Carton and Serjeant Stryver, the pushing and successful advocate for whom the other "devilled." Stryver, we gather from Edmund Yates's *Reminiscences*, was modelled by Dickens, from Mr. Edwin James, Q.C., who at one time "stood high in popular favour," and who "liked talking." There is plenty of subsequent moderate drinking —in Defarge's wine-shop principally—but with the exception of these two advocates, Stryver and Carton—" what the two drank together, between Hilary Term and Michaelmas might have floated a king's ship "—nobody appears to swallow an undue amount of alcohol, in this the most powerful, and the saddest, of all Dickens's books.

I could never wade through *Our Mutual Friend*, and *Little Dorrit* is not one of my favourite books. It was ruthlessly mauled by the *Saturday Review* soon after its appearance, and Thackeray's openly expressed opinion of the work was " *Little D.* is Deed stupid." I have

heard another great man express the same opinion
of it, in more elegant language.   There is not
much revelry in *Little D.* until we get to the
second volume ; and with the exception of
Blandois the strangler and the romantic Flora
nobody appears to have a really good thirst.   In
the Marshalsea the " collegians " were evidently
worse provided with alcoholic comfort than in
the Fleet ; and this is all which can be written
in this chapter about *Little Dorrit.*

Nicholas Nickleby, on the other hand, is full of
allusions to the flowing bowl.   Most of the
characters—Smike being a notable exception—
moisten their clay in some way or other, from
dear old Crummles, who is introduced to our
notice with a rummer of hot brandy-and-water
in one hand, to the ruffian Squeers.   Newman
Noggs owed his fall in life to the bold, bad,
bottle, and Mantalini presumably took to gin
together with the washer-woman, in his declining
years.   The Brothers Cheeryble were evidently
the right sort of people to dine with—although
their dinner-hour would hardly suit the present
generation—especially if they had many magnums
of that famed "Double Diamond."   Sir Mulberry
Hawk and his lordly victim drank deep, after the
fashion of the day ; whilst the keeper of the
" rooge-a-nore from Paris " booth on Hampton
race-course stimulates the energies of his patrons
with excellent champagne, port, sherry, and
(most likely) British brandy.   Old Gride keeps
a bottle of " golden water "—presumably the
Dantzic liqueur, " Acqua d'Oro," mentioned in
my chapter on that form of fluid—in his cupboard,

and doles out on one occasion a minute glass thereof to Newman Noggs, who would evidently, like the farmer at the audit dinner, prefer it "in a moog." Mr. Lillyvick, the collector of water-rates, was especially partial to punch—which was "cut off" so unexpectedly for the benefit of Nicholas, after his walk from Yorkshire to the metropolis ; and the whole of Mr. Crummles's company, ladies included, liked a taste of the same beverage. Finally, John Browdie, the good genius of the book, was a fellow of infinite swallow, always ready for his meals, and never behindhand when there was a full jug or bottle handy. And it is recorded that upon being knocked up by Nicholas, on the visit of the last-named to Yorkshire, with the news of Squeers's trial and sentence, "forced him down upon a huge settle beside a blazing fire, poured out from an enormous bottle about a quarter of a pint of spirits, thrust it into his hand, opened his mouth, and threw back his head as a sign to him to drink it." And before breakfast, too !

Bill Sikes, on occasion, drank brandy "at a furious rate " ; but more often poverty prevented his slaking his thirst on anything more deadly than Spitalfields ale, or eleemosynary gin. The whole of Mr. Fagin's pupils drank whenever opportunity offered, either malt liquor or gin-and-water out of pewter pots ; but the Jew himself, with the innate caution of his race, avoided the wiles of the bowl. Nancy was an " habitual," in her youth, most probably, or she would not have chummed up with such a criminal crew ; and as for Monks, the disorder known as *delirium*

tremens was no stranger to him. Bumble and
his wife were not averse to a social glass ; and
even the charity-boy, Noah Claypole, indulged,
during the absence of his master, the undertaker,
in oysters, porter, and some sort of wine, name
not mentioned. As far as we are told, the decent
members of society in *Oliver Twist* were very
moderate in their potations ; although it is in my
mind that Mr. Fang, the stipendiary, was a
port-wine man.

In *The Old Curiosity Shop* we get allusions to
liquids of all kinds, from orange-peel and water,
the favourite beverage of the Marchioness, to the
truly-awful "wanities" of Quilp, which took the
form of over-proof rum, boiled, burnt brandy, or
raw Schiedam out of a keg. Quilp, by the way,
if amusing enough, is the most exaggerated
character ever invented by the great novelist, and
has no business out of the realms of pantomime.
But he was very, very funny, as impersonated by
"Johnny" Clarke in the long ago. Dick
Swiveller was a swindler by profession, although
like many of these a boon companion, speechifier,
and framer of jovial sentiments. The "rosy
wine" was represented at his humble home by
geneva-and-water, and his astonishment when
Mr. Brass' lodger made a brew of "extraordinary"
rum-and-water in "a kind of temple, shining as
of polished silver," at the same time cooking a
steak, an egg, and a cup of coffee, in the same
temple, can only have been exceeded by his joy
at getting something really decent to drink.

The strolling performers with whom Nell
and Grandfather travelled did themselves par-

ticularly well, especially dear old Mrs. Jarley, whose consideration for her own comforts was fully equalled by her desire for the worldly welfare of others.

In *Bleak House* allusions to the bowl are infrequent. The rag-shop " Lord Chancellor " cremated himself with the aid of gin, and Mr. Tulkinghorn had a weakness for old port. Mr. Bucket favoured brown sherry, and Harold Skimpole would nibble a peach and sip claret, with an execution in his house. This is one of the best characters drawn by Dickens ; and although the type is not a familiar one, I have met him in the flesh.

Dombey and Son is by no means a " thirsty " work ; though Joey Bagstock was a votary of the bowl, like old Mrs. Brown. The rest of the company put together (I except "the Chicken") would not have enabled a publican to pay his rent, and one of the most melancholy parts of the book is the mention made therein of only one bottle of the old Madeira remaining in the cellar of Sol Gills, at a time when most of the other characters in the book—male and female—are making use of his house.

Next to my *Pickwick* I love my *Great Expectations*. Brandy-and-tar-water, imbibed by Pumblechook, in mistake, at the Christmas dinner, should properly come under the heading of " Strange Swallows " ; but the capacity of those two bottles of port and sherry, which he brought as a present on that occasion, has always been a puzzle to me. Joe, probably, would not be allowed more than a glass, and, naturally,

little Pip would be out of it ; but there remained
Wopsle, Mr. and Mrs. Hubble, and Pumblechook
himself ; whilst afterwards the sergeant joined
in the treat, and had two glasses.   And all these
people were served from one bottle ; for we are
distinctly told that the second cork was not
drawn until the first bottle had been emptied.

Miss Havisham's relations having been brewers,
beer was naturally the refreshment offered to
little Pip, whilst in service there, although there
seems to have been a bottle or two of wine in
the cellars, for the benefit of Mr. Jaggers and
others.   That worthy, like most successful
lawyers of the present day, was a light luncher—
a sandwich, and the contents of a flask of sherry
serving him for the purpose ; but we are told
that at his dinners both meat and drink were
unexceptionable.   His great hand always savoured
of scented soap, and at luncheon the odour of
superior sherry pervaded his office.

The convict's emissary, himself a released
felon, stirred his rum-and-water with a file ; and
this appears to have been the favoured drink of
the " returned transport," Magwitch.   There
was a large consumption of port and sherry—
chiefly by Pumblechook—after the remains of
Mrs. Gargery had been consigned to the earth ;
and what with frequent visits, on the part of the
inhabitants of those parts, to " The Jolly Barge-
men " and " The Boar," the landlords of those
establishments must have done a thriving trade
indeed.

I wonder if Sir Wilfrid Lawson, or any other
eminent abstainer, ever picked up a volume of

the *Pickwick Papers* for the purpose of perusal?
If so, and it was an illustrated edition, the frontis-
piece must have made his heart quail; for it
represents Pickwick himself standing on a chair
addressing a more or less excited audience, all
seated at a long table, and each with a cigar or
pipe in his mouth, and a large tumbler in front
of him. And if the eminent abstainer cared to
carry his researches farther, he would discover
that ere the Pickwickian deputation had started
on their first journey they had taken part in a
street fight, eventually quelled by the arrival of
a perfect stranger, who celebrates the occasion
by calling for glasses round of brandy-and-water,
hot and strong!

The *Pickwick Papers* absolutely reek with
alcohol, from title-page to name and address of
printer. Everybody drinks with everybody else,
both in and out of the Fleet Prison. The hospitality
of the good people is unbounded, and good and
bad alike do it full justice. The very instant
the belated travellers have crossed the threshold
of Dingley Dell they are fed with cherry brandy.
The entire deputation has "Katzenjammer,"
on the morning after their arrival at Rochester,
and a duel, or an attempted one, is the consequence.
In coffee-room, bar-parlour, or smoking-room,
an introduction, a story, or a song is an excuse
for a bowl of punch. Wherever the Pickwickians
go they carry trouble, more or less amusing to
the reader, and the trouble is invariably followed
by revelry.

That two medical students should wash down
their oysters with neat brandy — and before

breakfast—seems at the first glance an impossibility ; but many of those who know for certain the effects of undue indulgence are the most careless in indulging, and Bob Sawyer and his still more rascally friend and fellow-student Ben Allen are reckless types of a reckless profession. The same meal—oysters *cum* brandy—is partaken of, later on, by Solomon Pell and the coachman ; and Dickens probably knew that lawyers and stage-drivers, like sailors, can digest anything.

The most drunken man in the book, " the Shepherd," is an alleged teetotaller ; and the abstaining division will assuredly never forgive Dickens for his word-painting of Stiggins, whose " vanity " was pine-apple rum with hot water and plenty of sugar. The Wellers, *père et fils*, were not conservative in their potations ; and whether " the inwariable" is Wellerese for brandy hot, or rum hot, I am still uncertain, although many correspondents have sought to enlighten me on the subject ; said correspondents being anything but unanimous. One of the most favoured beverages mentioned in the work is "cold punch," by which I understand milk-punch, a very " more-ish " draught indeed.

I have prolonged this chapter perhaps unduly. But the subject of the Drinks of Dickens is too important a one to slur over. The man who cannot appreciate *Pickwick* has never yet come my way. There is a peculiar charm about the book, a broad hospitality, an unbounded love of the good things of this life which must endear it to the hearts of true sons of Britannia, who will revel, on occasion, no matter what obstacles may be placed in their way. And this is the method of procedure, the potation being occasionally varied, which succeeded all the troubles of the friends :—

"So to keep up their good humour they stopped at the first roadside tavern they came to" —this was after the punch and pound incident— "and ordered a glass of brandy-and-water all round, with a magnum of extra strength for Mr. Samuel Weller."

CHAPTER XX

SWORN OFF !

Introduction of temperance into England—America struck it
first—Doctor Johnson an abstainer—Collapse of the Permissive Bill—Human nature and forbidden fruit—Effects of
repressive legislation—Sunday closing in Wales—Paraffin for
miners—Toasting Her Majesty—A good win—A shout and
a drink — Jesuitical logic of the prohibitioners — The end
justifies the means—A few non-alcoholic recipes—Abstainers
and alcohol — Pure spring-water *v.* milk-punch — " Tried
baith ! "

THE first temperance society in England was
formed at Bradford, Yorkshire, on the 2nd
February 1830, the chief mover having been
Mr. Henry Forbes, who had signed the pledge
at Glasgow. But the use of ardent spirits was
condemned by many medical practitioners early
in the seventeenth century, although the United
Kingdom does not seem to have abstained from
strong waters any the more. Repressive legislation, in order to inculcate sobriety, was tried in
Massachusetts, U.S., early in the present century,
but a few years before a society had been formed
at Moreau, New York State, in order to prohibit
the consumption of both wines and spirits, except

medicinally, or wine except at public dinners or
in the Lord's Supper.

The work whence I have gleaned the above
details also informs the reader that "such as
Doctor Samuel Johnson and John Howard set
an example of abstinence from all inebriating
drinks"; which, as far as Doctor Johnson is
concerned, is somewhat startling news to myself.
I had always imagined that the burly lexico-
grapher—I was reproved by a critic for calling
him this in *Cakes and Ale*—was a bit of a boon
companion ; and the records of Fleet Street
taverns by no means tend to contradict this idea.
Not only is the hard, oaken seat at one end of
the dining-room of " Ye Olde Cheshyre Cheese "
marked with a brass plate, with a suitable inscrip-
tion, but the many visitors to that snug hostelry,
including hundreds of our American cousins, are
always taken upstairs and shewn Doctor Johnson's
chair.   Did "Sam," and " Davy," and " Noll "
slake their thirst on cold water, beneath that
tavern's roof?   I trow not.   Cross out Doctor
Johnson's name as a total abstainer, please.

In 1834, Mr. J. S. Buckingham, who was
returned for Sheffield to the first Reform Parliament, succeeded in obtaining a select committee
of the House of Commons, to enquire into the
causes, extent, and remedies of drunkenness.   In
the meantime the limitation of the pledge to
abstention from ardent spirits had proved a
greater drawback than in other countries, because
beer had been the popular beverage, and its use
a cause of widespread drunkenness before ardent
spirits were commonly sold.   But the idea of

our legislators before 1834 had been that " good malt and hops could injure nobody."

From '34 to '45 there was great activity in the temperance ranks throughout the world; and in '53 the United Kingdom Alliance for the Legislative Suppression of the Liquor Traffic was formed, its first president being Sir W. C. Trevelyan. In March '64 a Permissive Prohibitory Bill was brought into the House of Commons, but although repeatedly re-introduced it never obtained a second reading. Nor is it likely that such a Bill will ever become law as long as the sons of Britannia are living outside a state of slavery. Repressive legislation serves only to stimulate that which it claims to check; and thus it is that these would-be reformers, whether Prohibitors of the Drink Traffic, Vigilance and Purity Societies, and Anti-gambling Societies have succeeded in making the state of London infinitely worse, as regards drunkenness, chastity, and betting, than it was forty years ago.

Poor frail humanity will always do the thing which it ought not to do in preference to fulfilling its obligations. It has been so since the beginning of the world, and will continue so until the end. Forbidden fruit has ever been the sweetest; and it is characteristic of mankind—and more especially of womankind—to oppose, as far as they can, any attempt at restraint. What has been the effect of closing Cremorne Gardens, the Argyll Rooms, and other public resorts where dancing and revelry were carried on until the small hours, five-and-twenty years ago?

The evil took refuge in the open streets, and,
more recently, in so-called social clubs, in which
illicit liquors were, and are, sold, and the pander,
and the pimp, and the bully met, and meet the
drunkard, the dupe, and the greenhorn.   What
has been the effect of the Anti-gambling Cru-
sade?   To create working-men bookmakers.
This is a fact.   In most large warehouses and
factories there are *employés* who will lay "starting
prices," in shillings and sixpences, to their mates.
There is not a tithe of the amount wagered
amongst the upper classes that there was in the
fifties and sixties; but amongst the horny-handed
sons of toil the vice has increased to an enormous
extent, mainly owing to repressive legislation.
If a man wants to gamble there is only one
factor to prevent him—impecuniosity; and even
that factor need not prevent a man from having
a drink if he waits in the tap-room long enough
on pay-day.   Since Sunday closing in Wales,
shebeens have arisen by the hundred; and
paraffin, for want of a better drink, is still drunk
on the Sabbath day, by the miners in the
Rhondda Valley.

All honour to him who abstains from strong
drink for conscience' sake, or in the hope that
others may profit by his example.   But the lash
of scorn for him who because he does not
swallow fermented refreshment himself, says to
his brother " Thou shalt not drink !"   The
Puritans abolished bear-baiting, not on account of
the cruelty to the bears, but because the alleged
sport gave pleasure to the people; and the
Puritans of the day, who forbid cakes and ale,

and hunting, and horse-racing, do so ror the self-
same reason.

"He who does not smoke," said the sage,
"has known no great sorrow." Similarly, it
may be urged that he who never joins in a
friendly glass has known no great joy. Do we
express our unfeigned joy and thankfulness for
having a great and good Queen to reign over us
by toasting her in flat soda-water? Forbid the
deed! When our sons return from the midst of
many and great dangers, from the battle-field,
the raging deep, or the land of savages, do we
express our delight by putting the kettle on to
boil? Avaunt! I have known a man who had
won £27,000 on a certain Wednesday at Ascot,
dine that same night off a chump chop, chips,
and·a bottle of ginger-beer, at a coffee-house no
great distance from Fleet Street. And he gave
the waitress one penny for herself, and counselled
her not to "get gamblin'" with it. But
amongst my own personal friends, when the
fancied horse catches the eye of the judge, there
is revelry; and who shall say that they sin thereby? I do not believe in the man who takes his
winnings sadly—or at all events impassively. "A
shout, and a drink, and then sit down and write
about it," is the programme pursued by a journal-
istic friend; and although I do not always "write
about it," 'tis much the same programme pursued
by myself. Nor do we rejoice for the sole reason
that we have got the better of somebody else.
For, alas! the balance at the end of the year is far
too often in favour of that "somebody else."

"On the question of the prohibition of the

liquor traffic," says an authority on the ethics ot total abstinence, "there has been much controversy. Its opponents have contended that it is an invasion of personal liberty ; that even when imposed by a majority it is a violation of the rights of the minority ; and that all that is really required is such a magisterial and police supervision as will repress drunkenness as much as possible, and inflict different penalties on offenders. To this statement various answers are returned. With regard to the violation of personal liberty the prohibitionists maintain that in one sense all law interferes with liberty. A good law interferes with the liberty to do wrong. Therefore, they say, assuming that the common sale of drinks wrongs the public, a law interfering with this wrong is in accord with true liberty. They hold that individual profit must be subservient to the public welfare, *Salus populi suprema lex*. If hardship is alleged as affecting the buyer, the statement of John Stuart Mill is quoted, who declared that every artificial augmentation of the price of an article is prohibition to the more or less poor ; yet there is hardly any government which does not in some way or other legislate so that the price of intoxicants is increased. As to the possibility of extirpating intemperance by means of strict regulation as to the sale of drink, the prohibitionists affirm that the existing system has been tried for hundreds of years, and often under the most favourable circumstances for its success, and that yet the licensing system, as judged by its fruits, is confessed to be a melancholy failure."

My remarks on the above are few and simple.
It is this very Jesuitical logic which has earned
the " prohibitionists " the contempt of all friends
of freedom.   It is this false and tyrannical doc-
trine which asserts that "the end justifies the
means," which still stinks in the nostrils of the
majority of the people's representatives in
Parliament.

Now for a few hints as to some non-alcoholic
beverages. And first of all let it be stated that
the thirsty man can do much worse than turn to
a teetotal beverage—as long as he avoids the
bottled flatulence which is sold, and freely adver-
tised outside, in pretty nearly every country
cottage which can boast of good accommodation
for travellers, and a bicycle shed.   The iced
fruit-fizzers of Mr. Sainsbury—where the pick-
me-ups come from—close to the *Lady's Pictorial*
office, are, to my personal knowledge, freely
patronized in summer-time by habitual worshippers
at the shrine of Bacchus.   Moreover a follower
of the sport of kings would rather go without
whisky all the afternoon than miss his cup of
tea, after business hours.   No directions are
needed here for the manufacture of tea or coffee.
Every housewife has a way of her own ; and it
is as the laws of the Medes and Persians that her
way is the only way.   Nor need a discussion be
entered on as to the respective merits of different
brands of cocoa.

A Superior Lemon Squash.

Take the juice of eight lemons, and sweeten it,
allowing one tablespoonful of sifted sugar to each

lemon.   Put the juice into an enamelled saucepan
and simmer gently over the fire until the sugar is
quite dissolved.   Beat up the white of one egg, add
to the syrup, and stir well till the mixture boils ; let
it boil for a minute or two, and pour gently through
a jelly-bag into a basin.   When quite cold add a
quarter of an ounce of citric acid, bottle, and cork
tightly.   When required for use, put six drops of
Angostura bitters in a soda-water tumbler, turn it
round and round, then add a wine-glassful of the
squash, fill up with soda-water, place a thin slice of
lemon atop, and serve with two straws.

Almond Comfy.

Put six ounces of pulverized sweet almonds and
two ounces of smashed bitters ditto into a saucepan
with one quart of water, and let it simmer for a
quarter of an hour ; then add one pound of sifted
sugar.   When dissolved strain through a hair sieve or
jelly-bag, and add a tablespoonful of orange-flower
water.   When cold, a wine-glassful of the mixture
should be put into a tumbler, which should be filled
up with soda- or Seltzer-water.

Temperance Cider.

Put half a gallon of water on to boil, and when
boiling throw into the saucepan a dozen medium-
sized apples, cut into slices unpeeled.   Keep the
lot boiling until quite tender, then strain till dry,
taking care not to let any of the pulp escape through
the sieve.   Add sifted sugar *ad lib.*, and the juice of
two lemons.   Let the mixture stand until cool,
when it will be ready for use.   Of course ice is an
improvement, in warm weather.   And only add a
soupçon of *eau de vie* when you are quite alone.

The next item on the programme is called in my book,

Drink for Dog Days,

but as this is not a nice name, and suggests hydrophobia and—other things, I will re-christen it

Citron de Luxe.

The composition is very simple. Put a lemon-ice in a large tumbler, fill up with soda-water, stir well, and drink.

N.B.—Mr. George Krehl, of "Verrey's," who knows something about dog days, and dogs, won the prize offered in the *Sporting Times* for the best recipe for a summer drink, many years ago, with a similar suggestion. But G. K. added a small glass of Curaçoa, and (I think) a drop or two of Angostura bitters. ·

Cherry Cobbler

Take one pound of cherries of Kent, free from stalks and stones. Throw them into a pint of boiling syrup, made of one pound of loaf-sugar dissolved in one pint of water. Let the cherries boil as fast as possible—" gallop " is, I believe, the technical word—for ten minutes, and then add a quart of boiling water ; put the whole into a pan, and when cold strain. The addition of soda-water will make it all the more watery.

D. D.

[*This is not naughty language, but short for Delicious Drink.*]

Mix together one pint of raspberries, one pint of

strawberries, and one pint of white currants, all free
from stalks ; mash them well together, and then add
two quarts of boiling water, and three quarters of a
pound of sifted sugar.   Let the mixture remain in a
bowl all night—unless you make it early in the
morning, when all day will do as well—then strain,
and give it the dear children before their dinner.

Raspberry Squash.

Put into a large soda-water tumbler one tablespoonful of raspberry syrup, one tablespoonful of
lemon squash (*vide* above) and a lump of ice ; nearly
fill the glass with soda-water, and ornament with a
thin slice of lemon, and a few red and white raspberries.   Drink through straws.

Raspberry Vinegar.

Take ripe, dry raspberries, and pour over them
sufficient good malt vinegar to cover them ; let them
stand three or four days, stirring occasionally with a
silver spoon.   On the fourth day, strain through a
sieve, and let them drain for some hours ; measure
the juice, and add an equal quantity of sifted sugar ;
put into a lined preserving pan, and let the mixture
boil gently for five or six minutes.   Carefully remove
the scum as it rises.   When cold, bottle, and cork
well.   A wine-glassful with a bottle of soda-water
is a refreshing "cooler" in illness.

Elderberry Punch.

Put two bottles of elderberry wine, —— hallo !
what's this ?   I turn to the recipe for Elder Wine,
and read : "A quart of brandy thrown into the cask

when it is about to be sealed up will greatly improve the wine." Then what sort of a temperance drink can Elderberry Punch be ? No more on that head, in the name of St. Wilfrid.

I also read, in the work of reference from which I am quoting, under the same heading, "Temperance Drinks," that :—

"Many of the British wines, mixed with an equal quantity of water, with a little ice, make very cool and refreshing drinks." Very, very likely. But can there be wine without fermentation ? And are the total abstainers, not content with drinking alcoholic gingerade and stone ginger-beer, getting the wedge in still further. Forbid it !

Cold Spring-water

is a most excellent drink, and according to so great an authority as Sir Henry Thompson, not only the cheapest drink in the world but the best. For my own poor part I prefer milk-punch. And as the Scotchman said, I have "tried baith."

INDEX OF RECIPES

R

THE END

Printed by R. & R. Clark, Limited, *Edinburgh.*

www.ingramcontent.com/pod-product-compliance
Lightning Source LLC
Chambersburg PA
CBHW030513100426
42813CB00001B/19